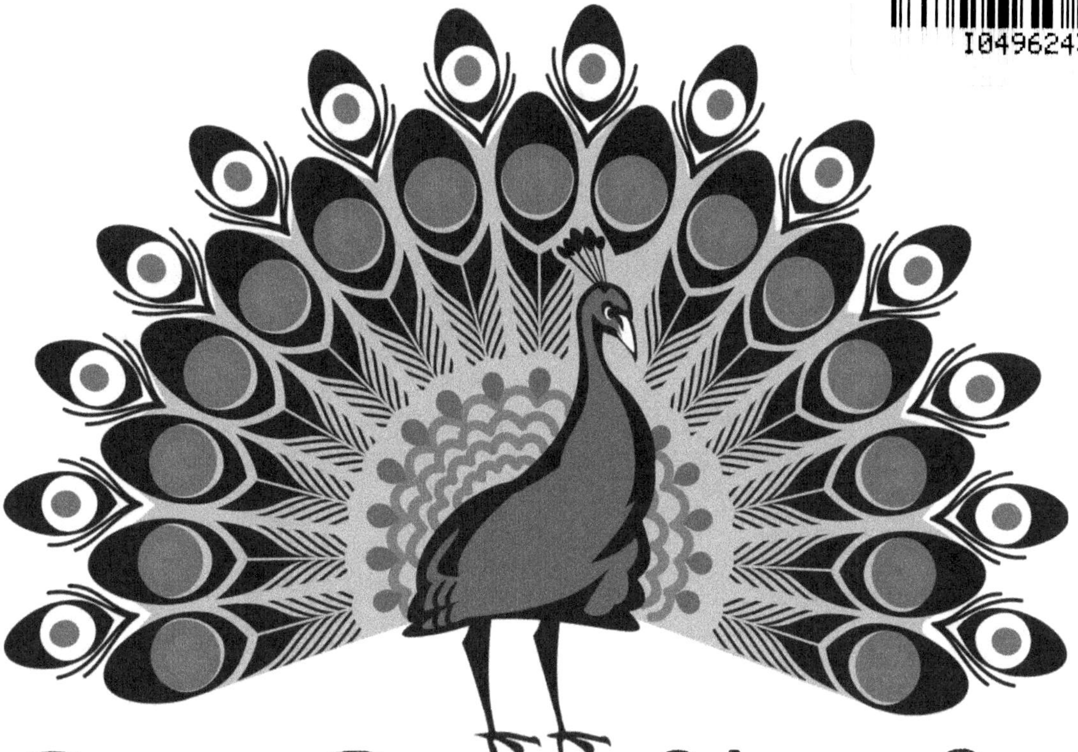

A Bird Does Not Sing Because It Has An Answer.
It Sings Because It Has
A Song.

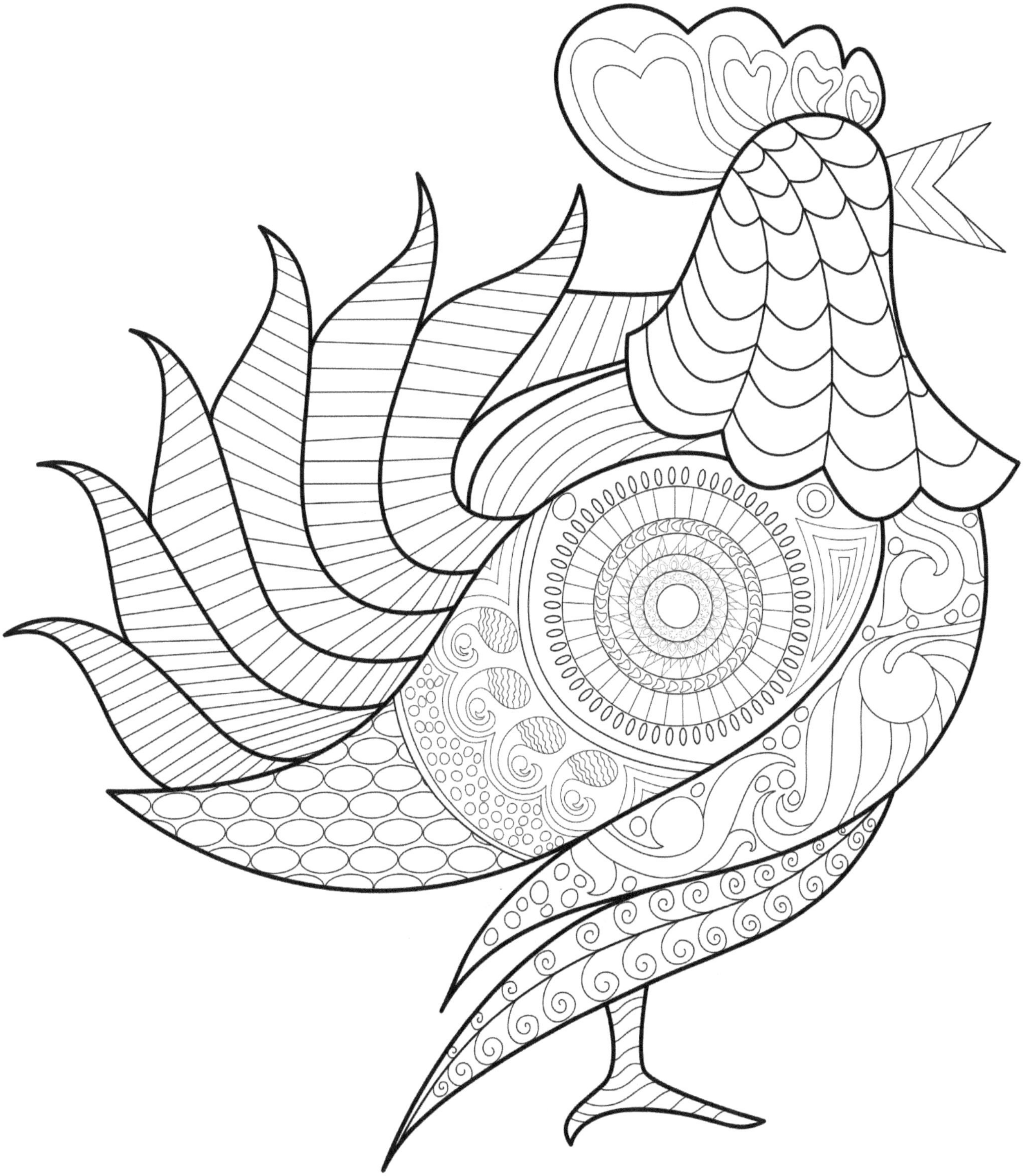

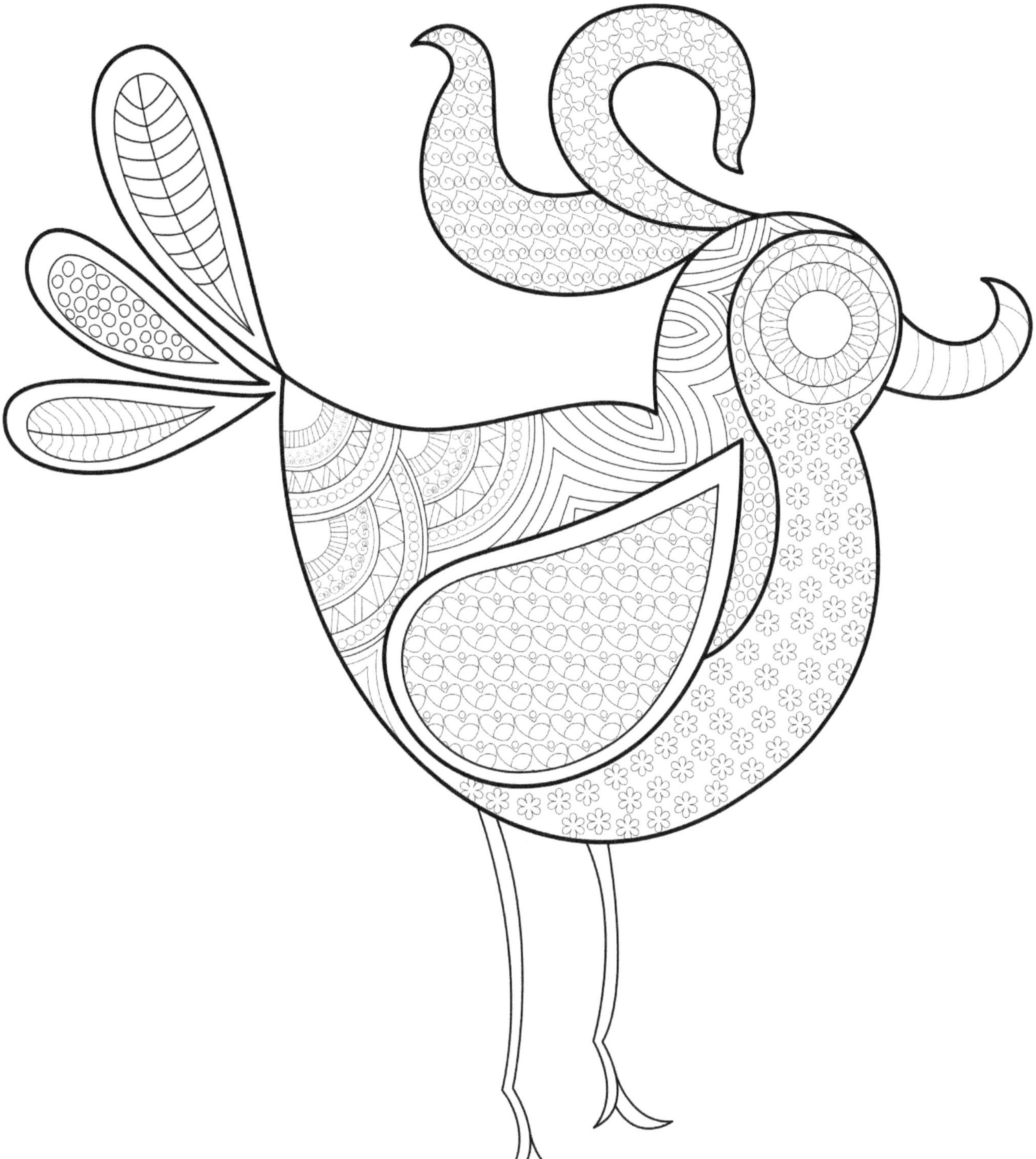

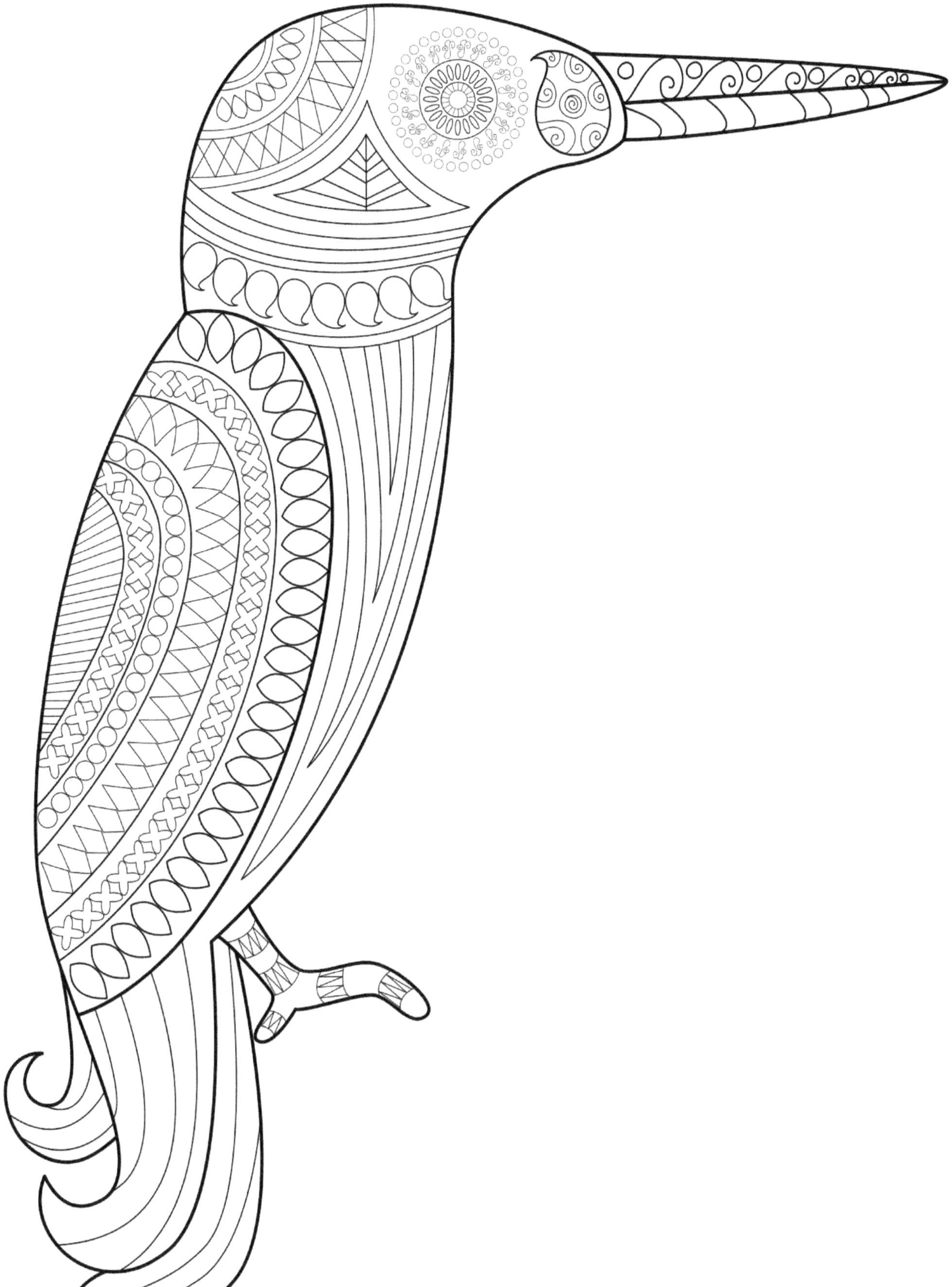

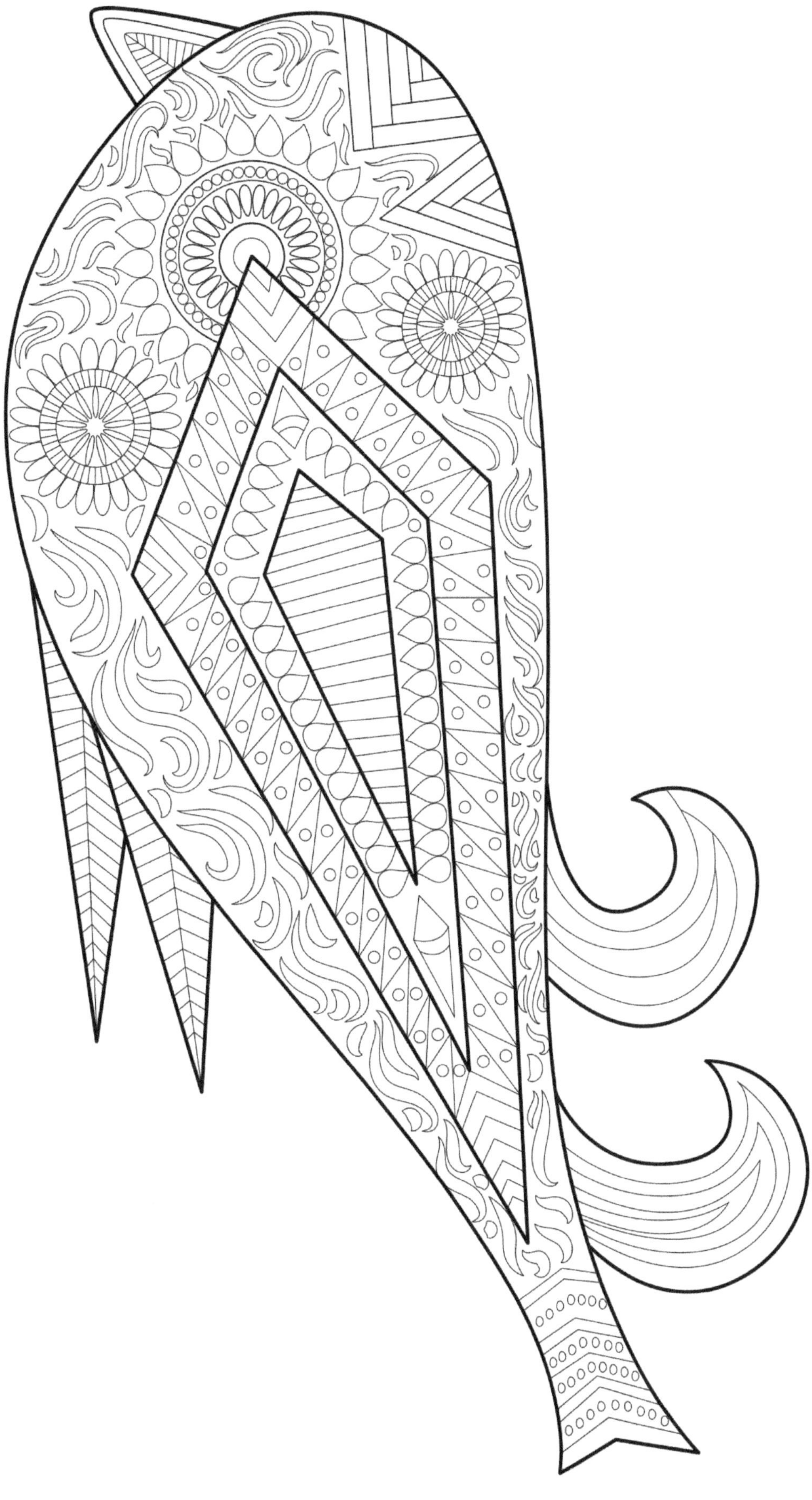

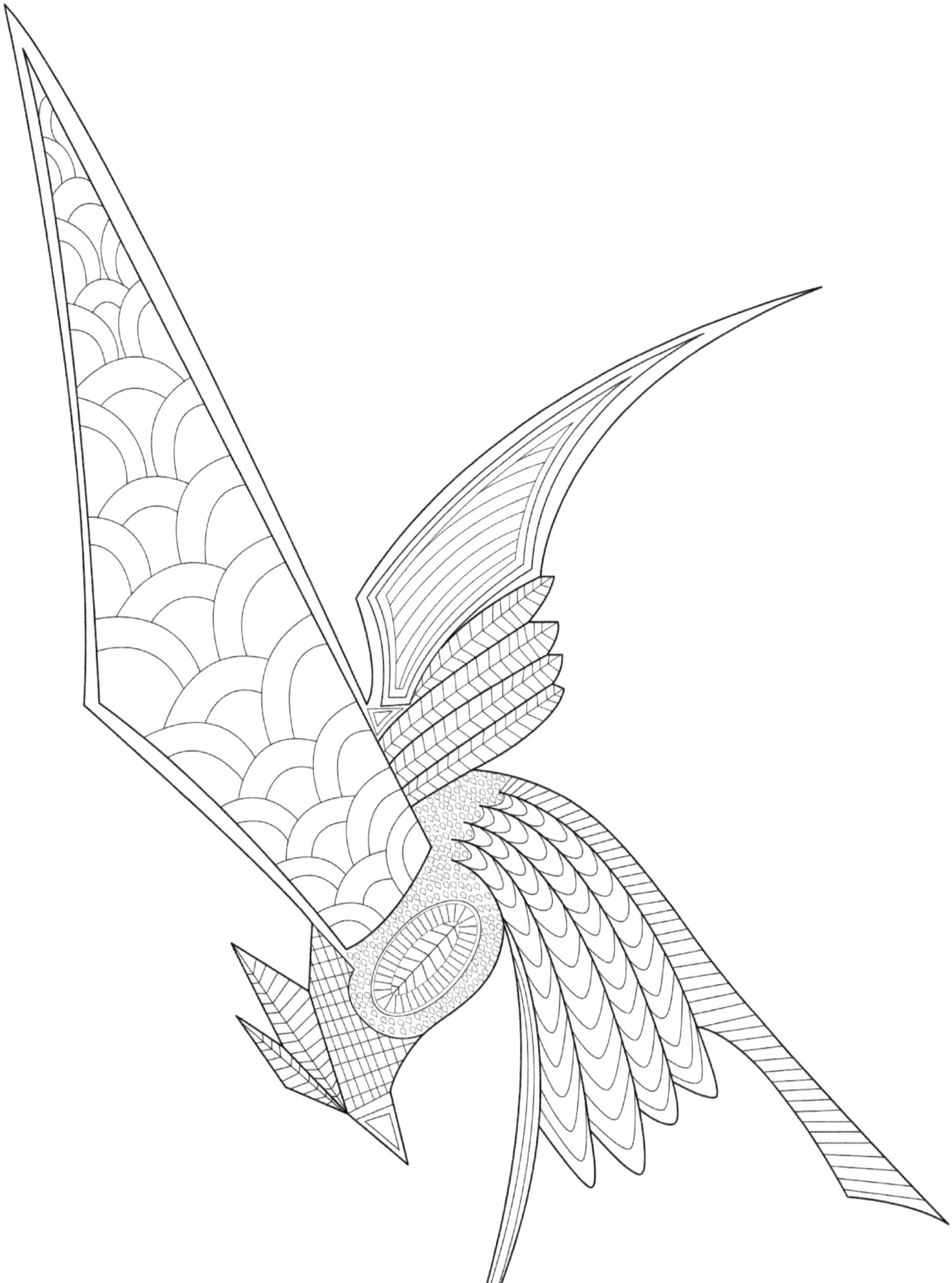

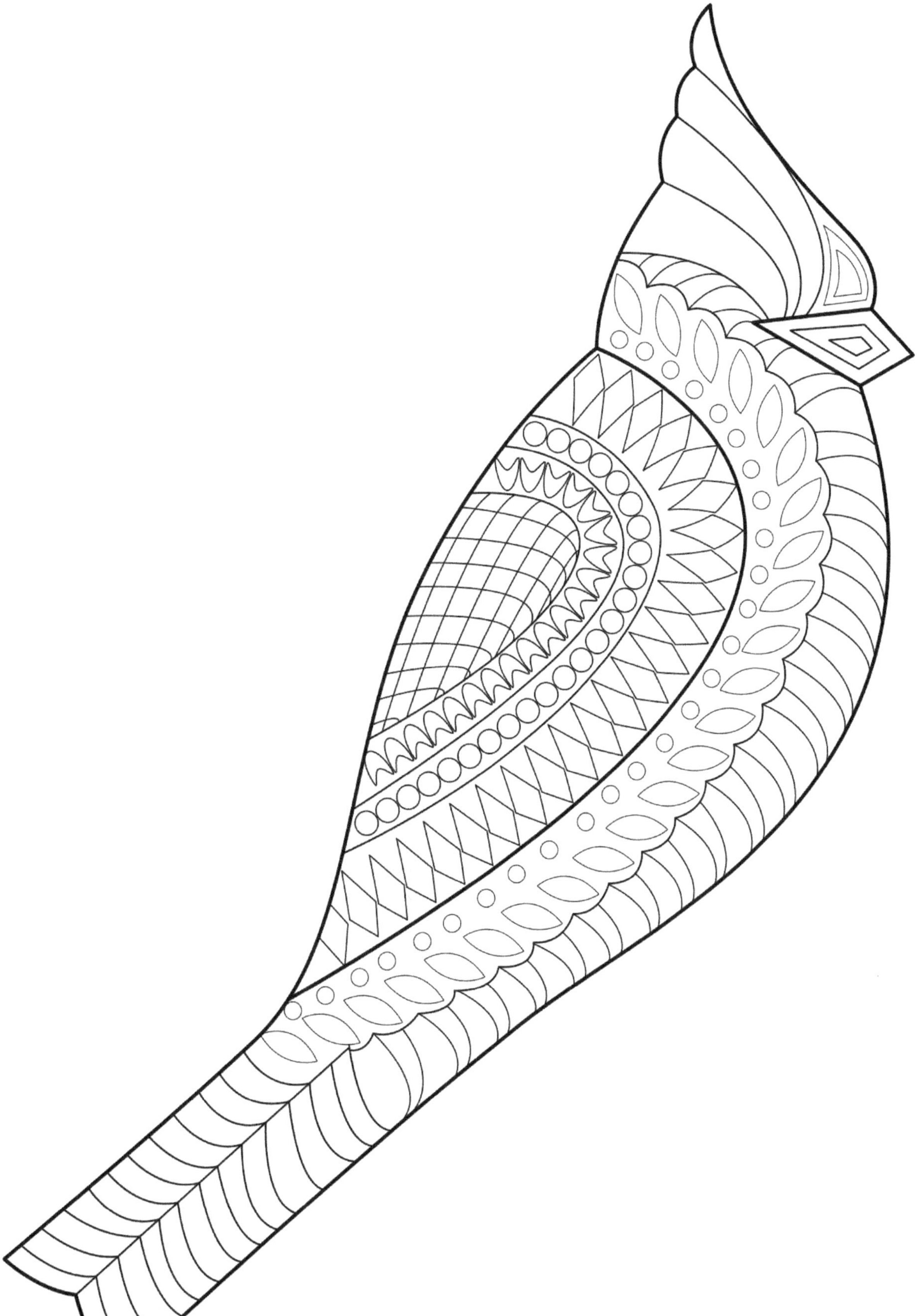

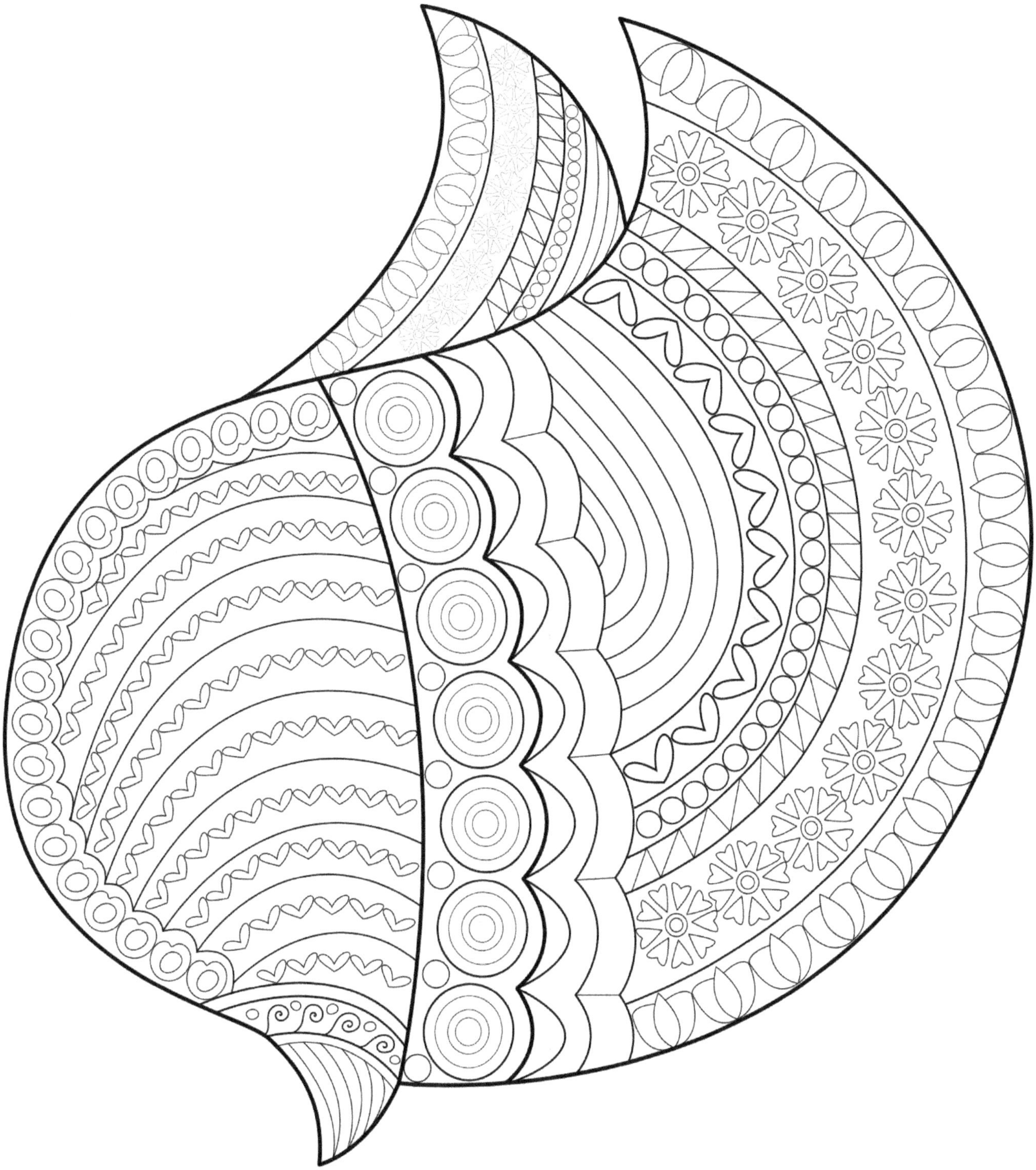

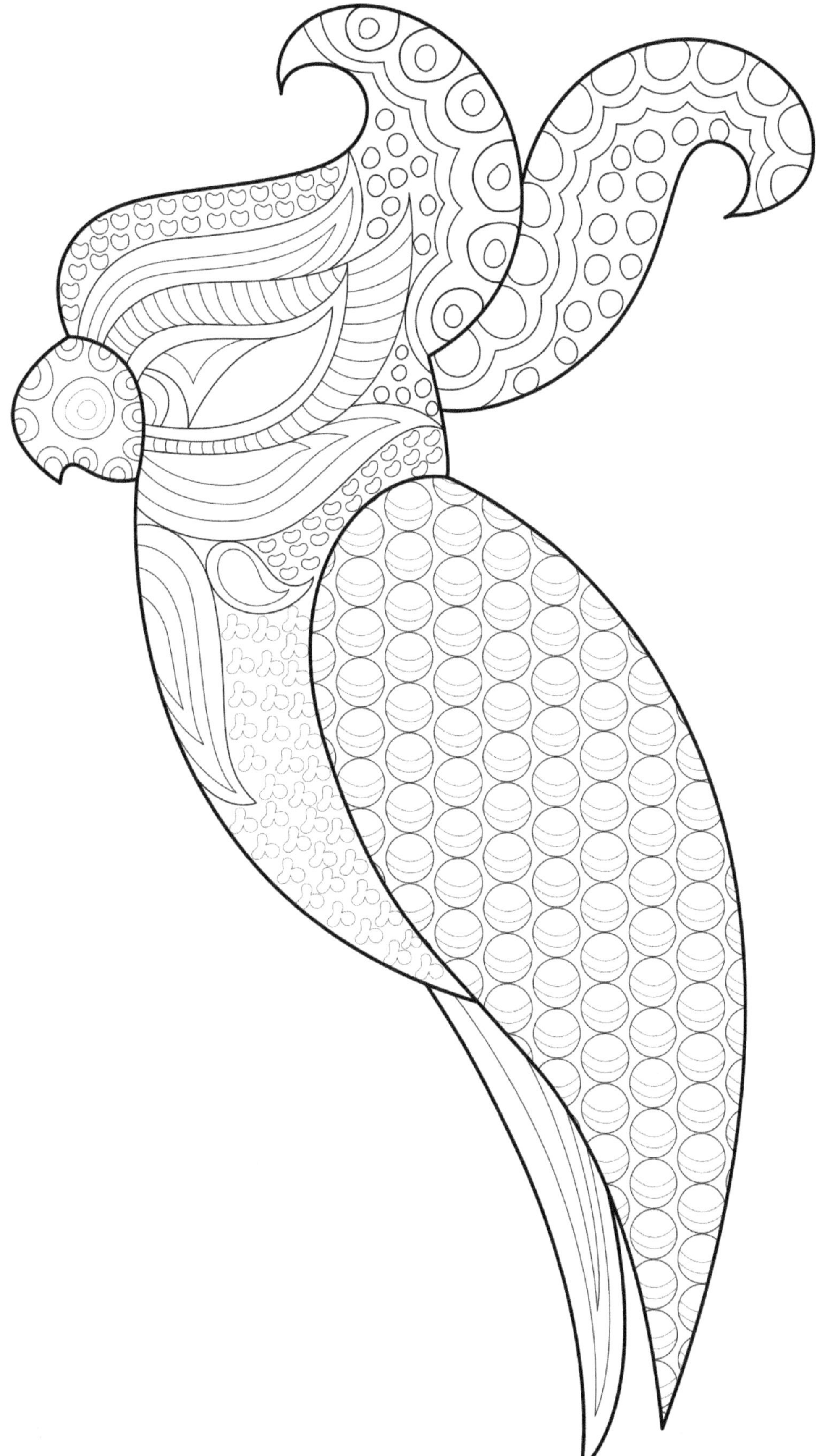

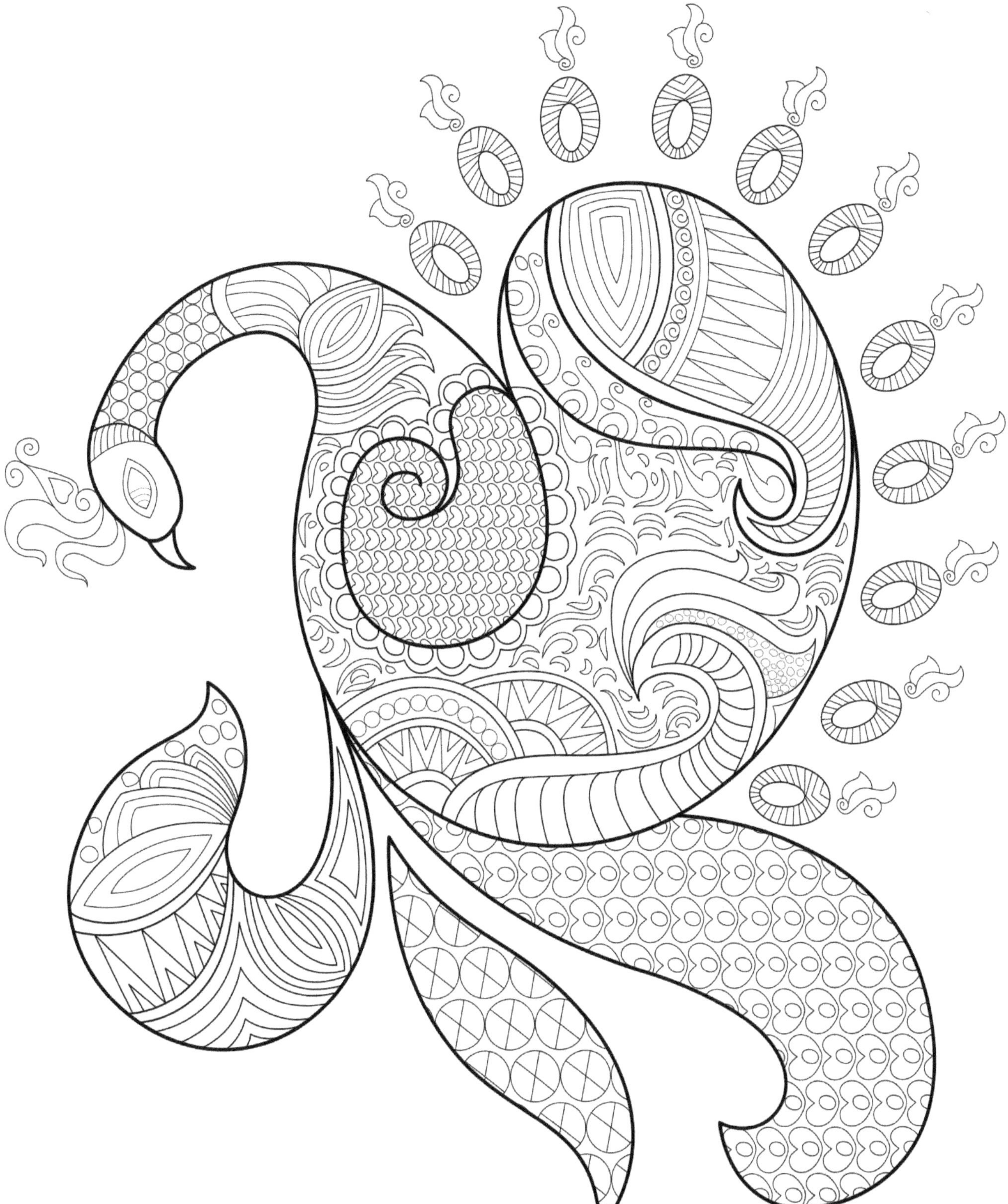

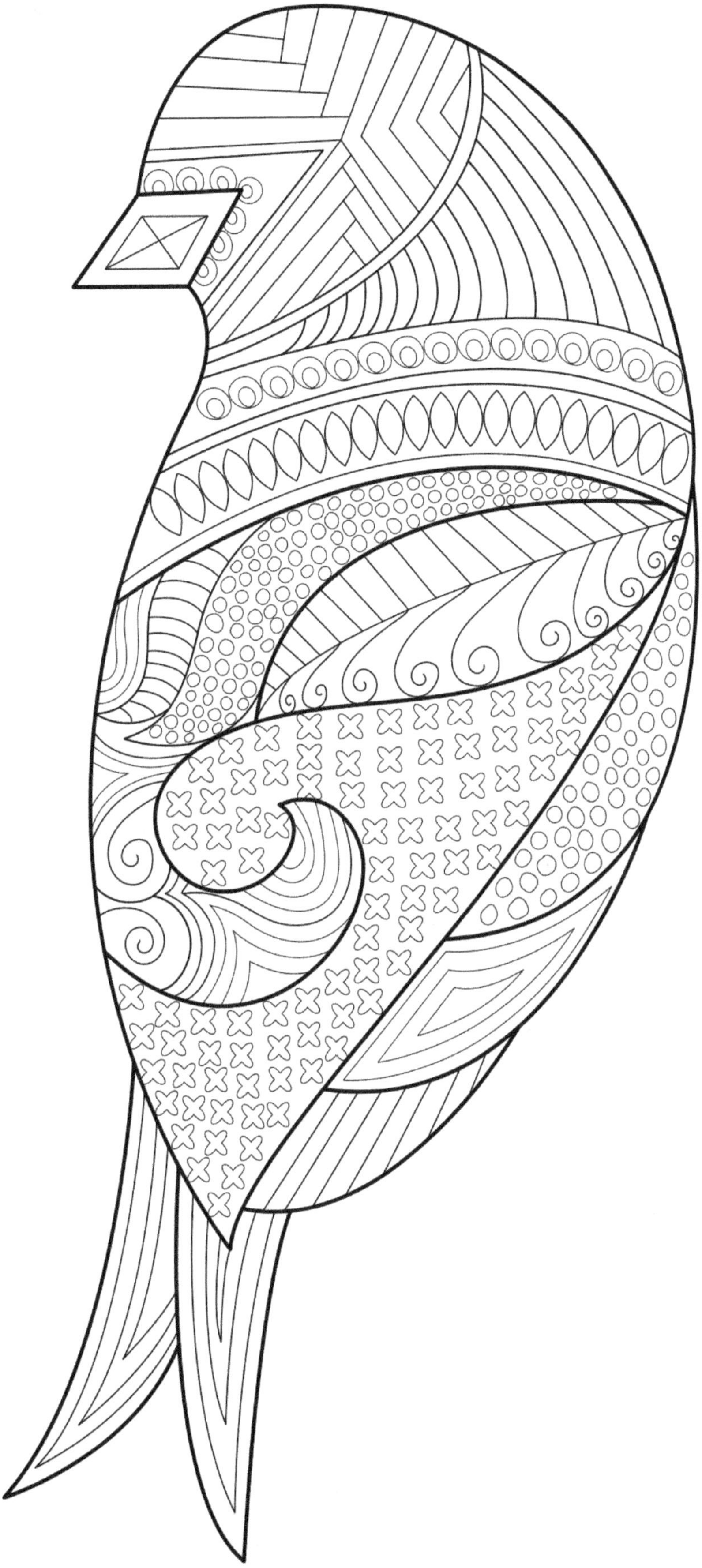

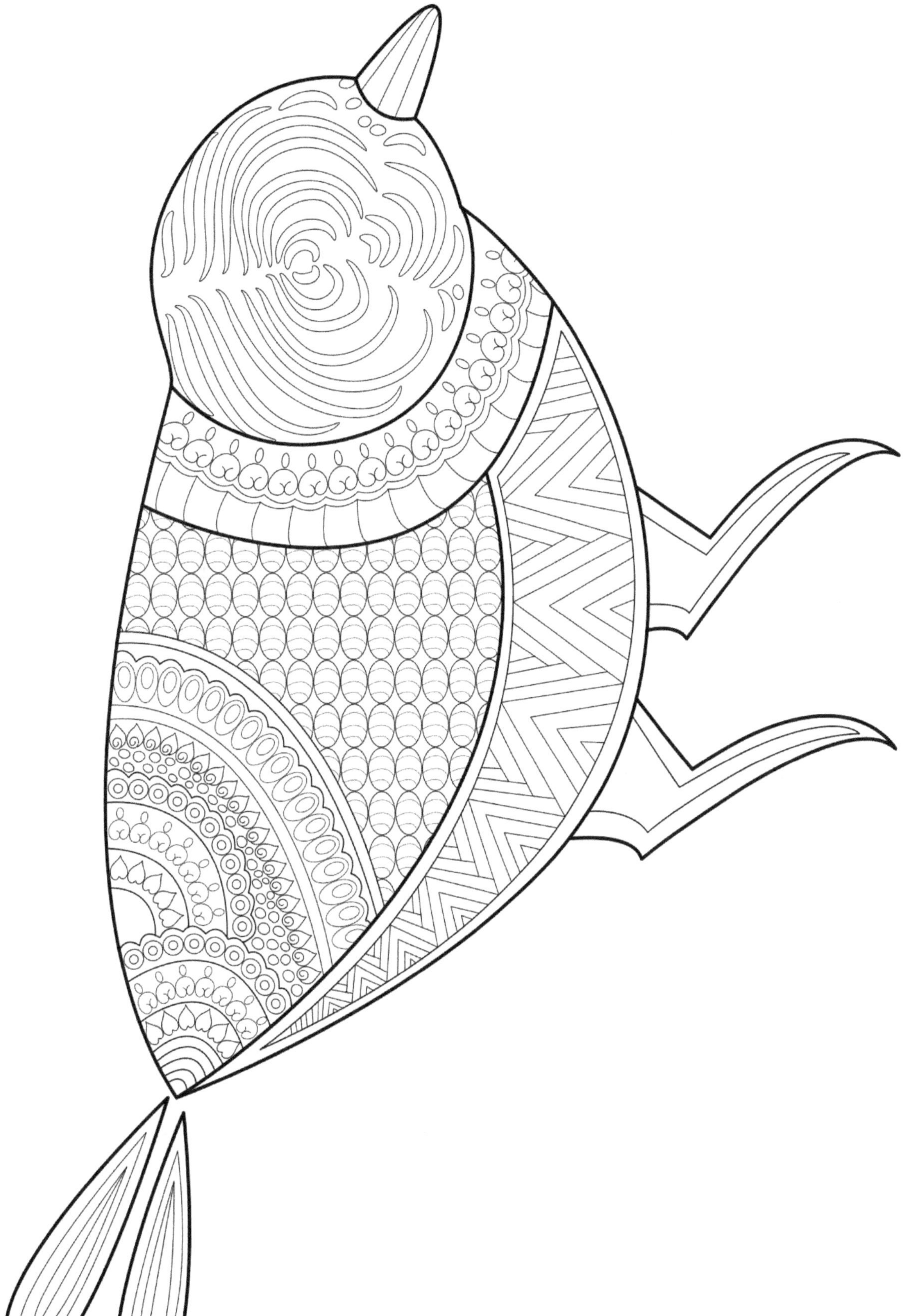

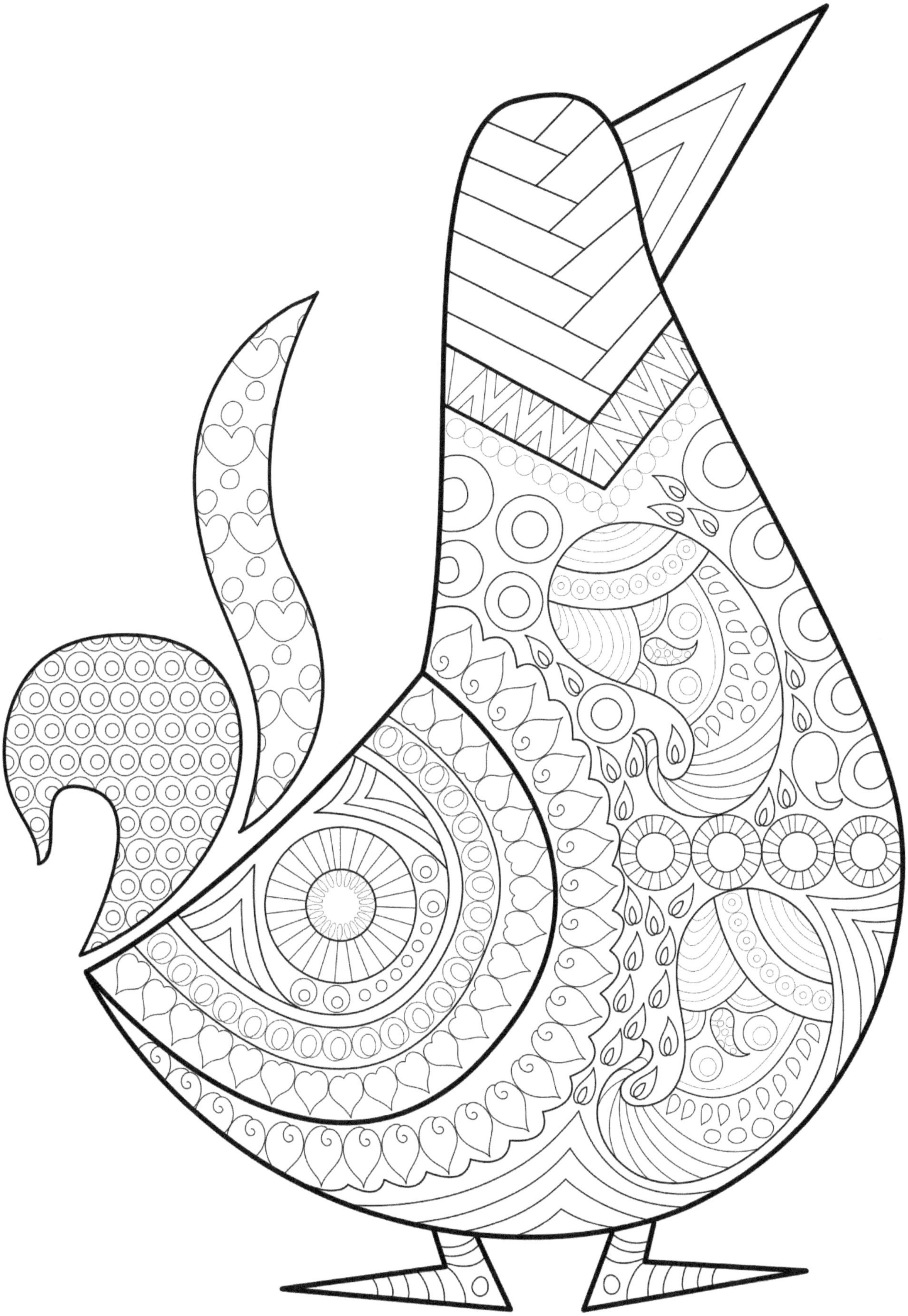

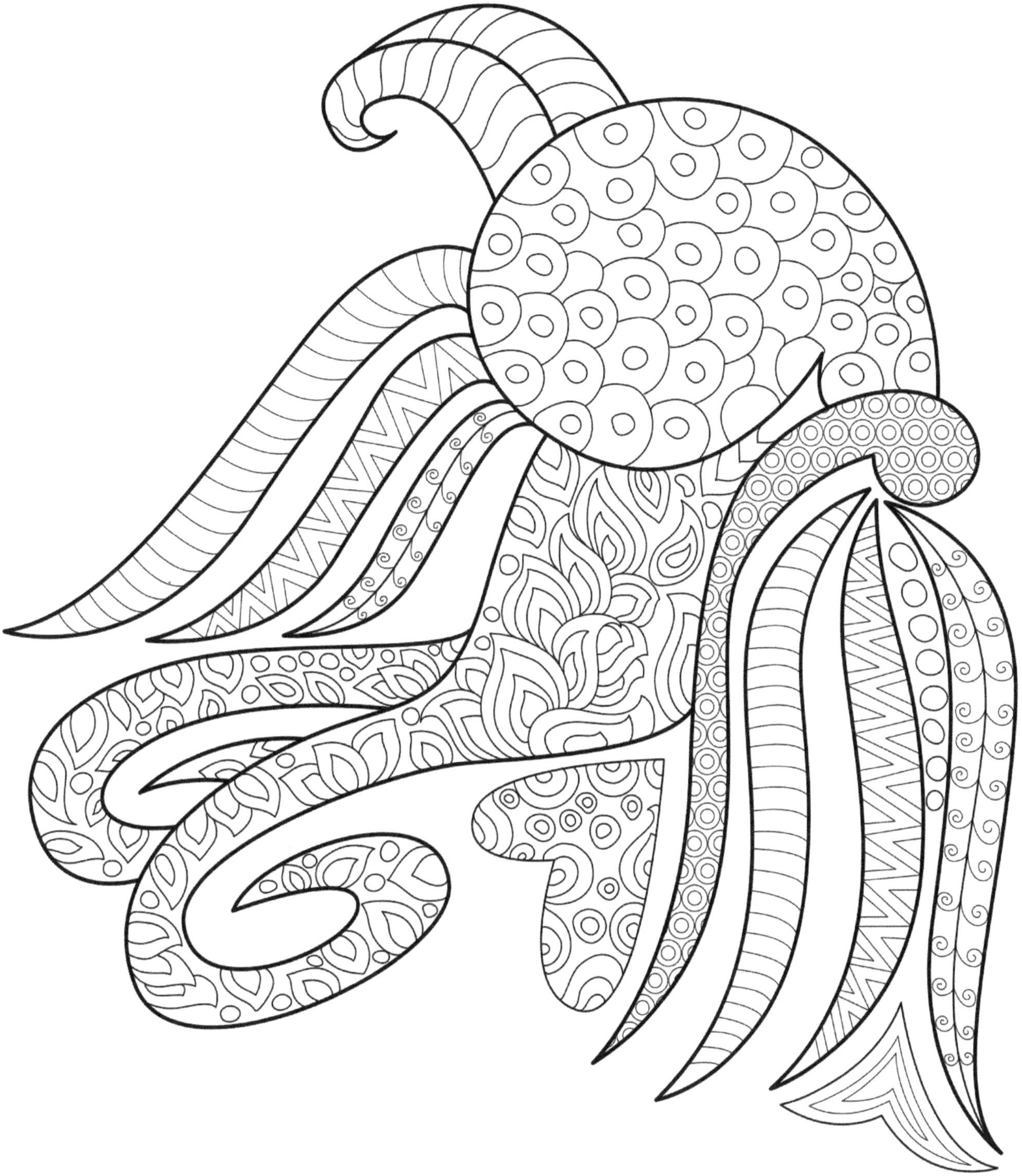

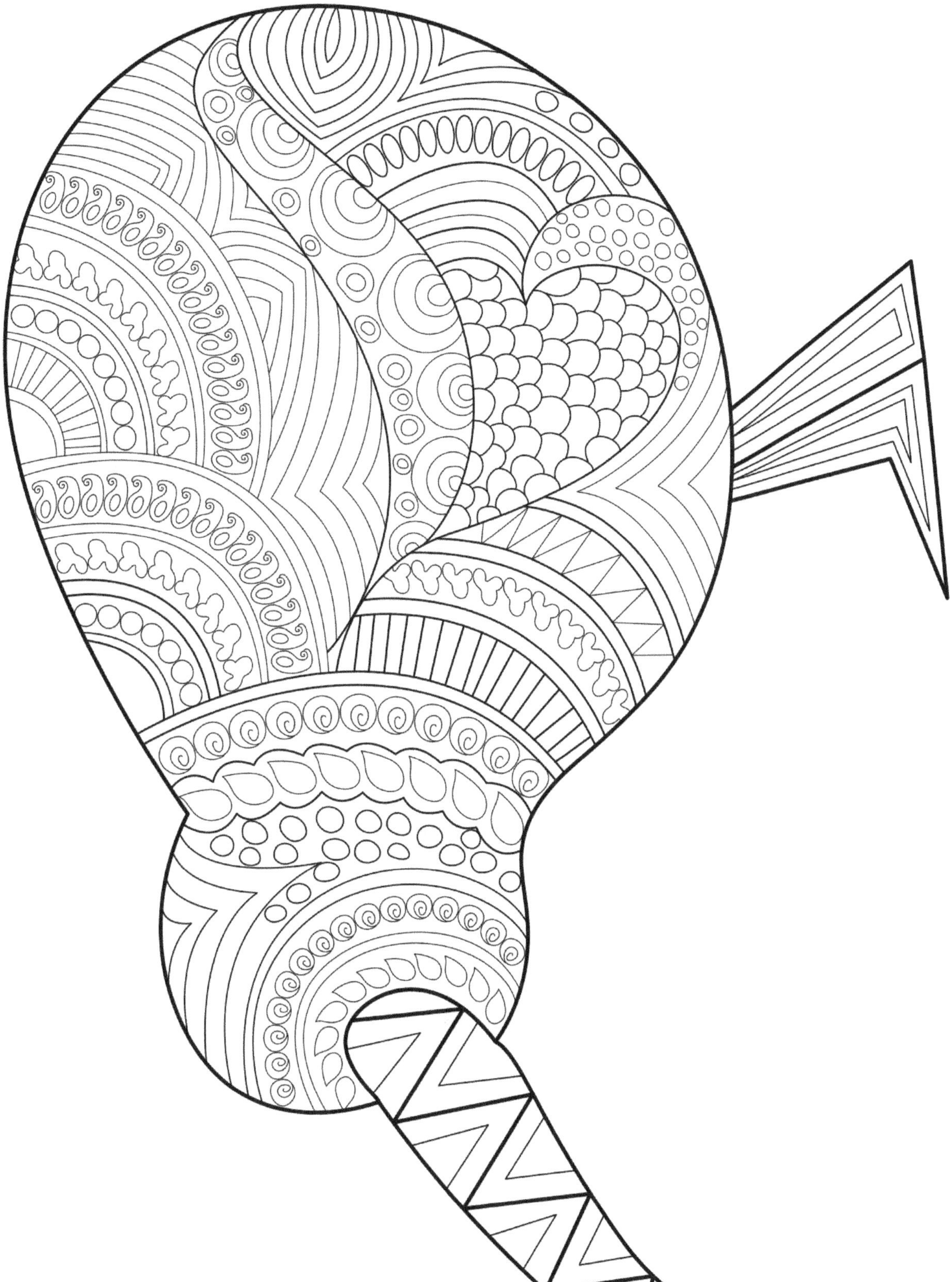

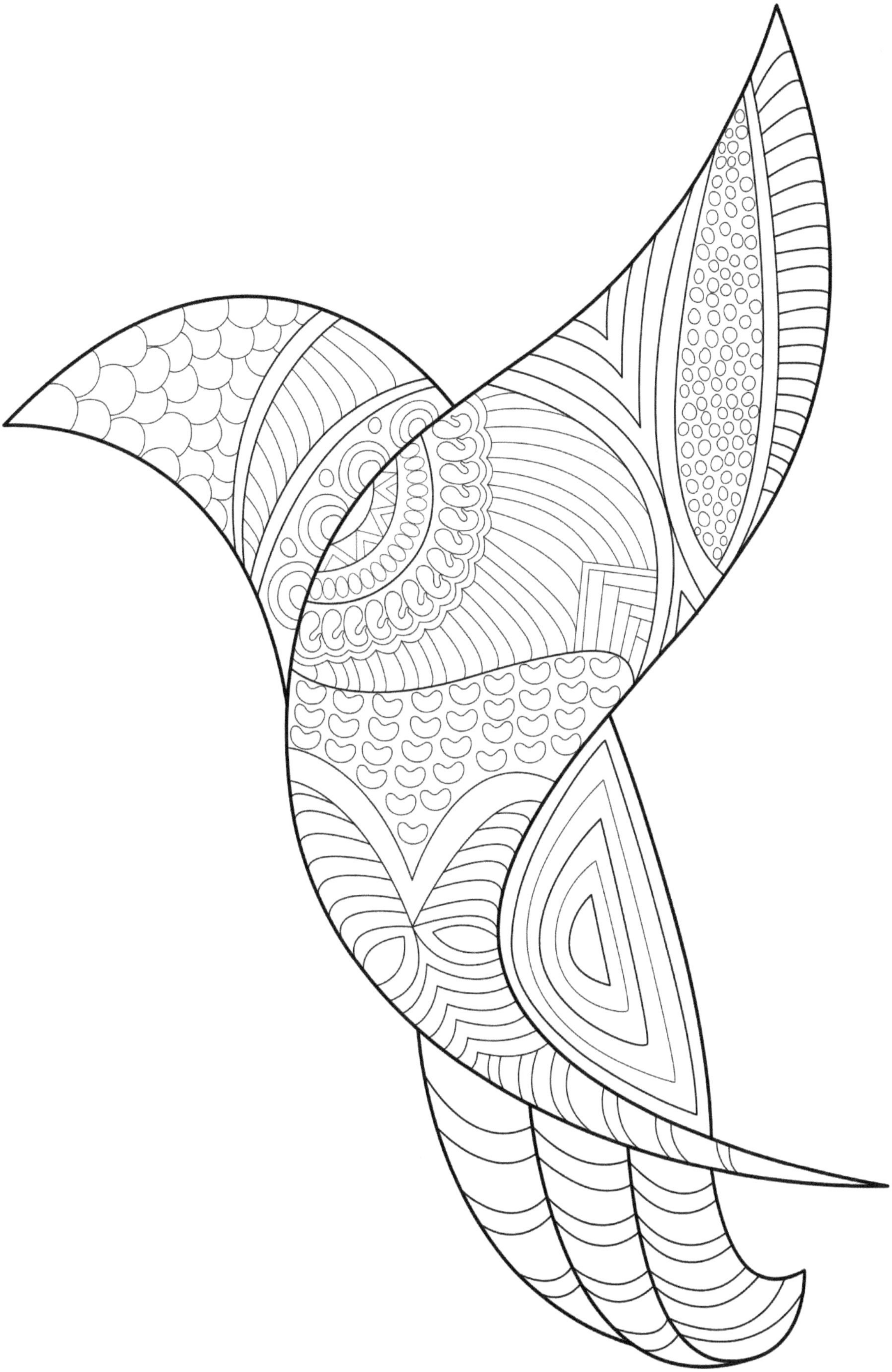

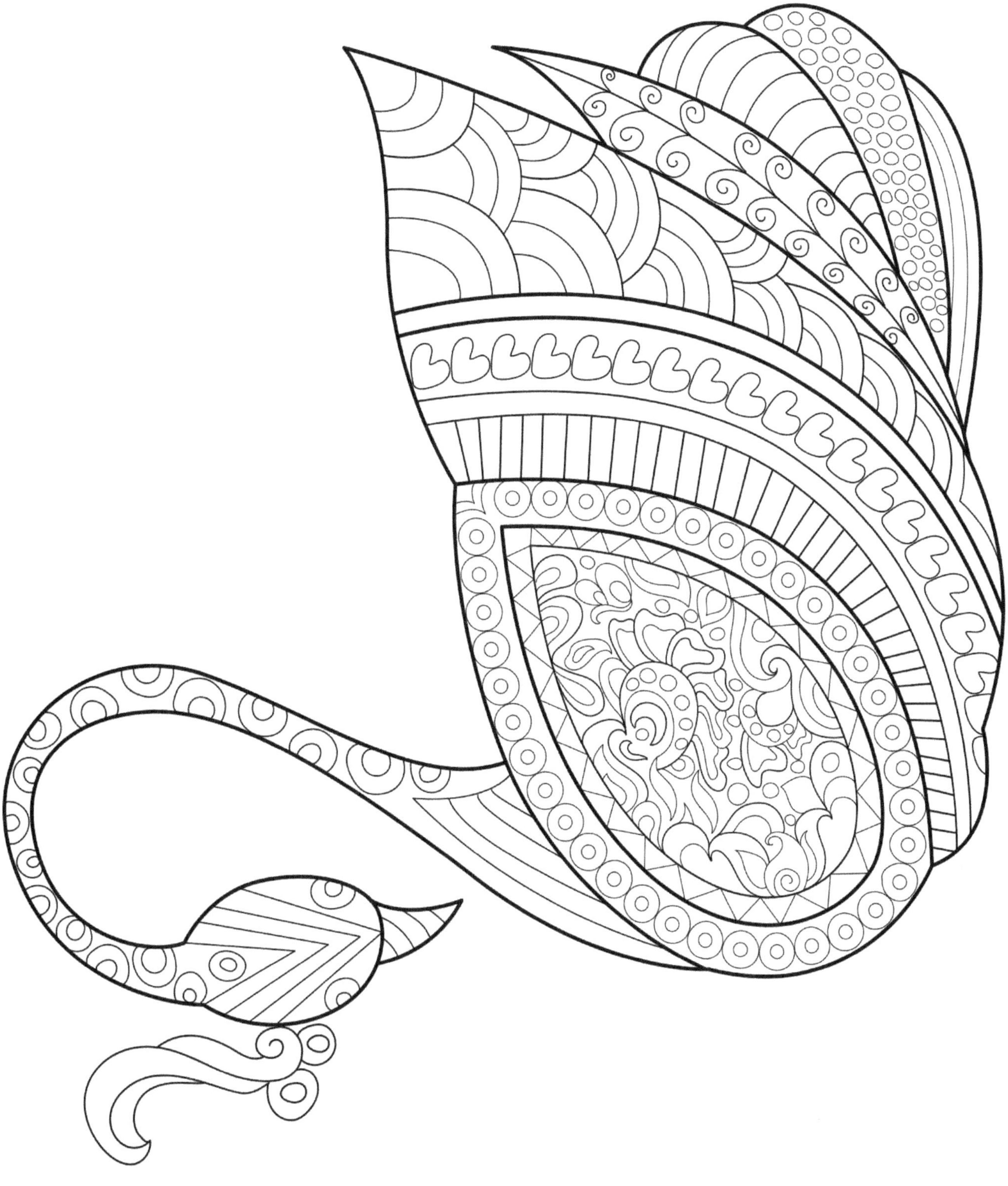

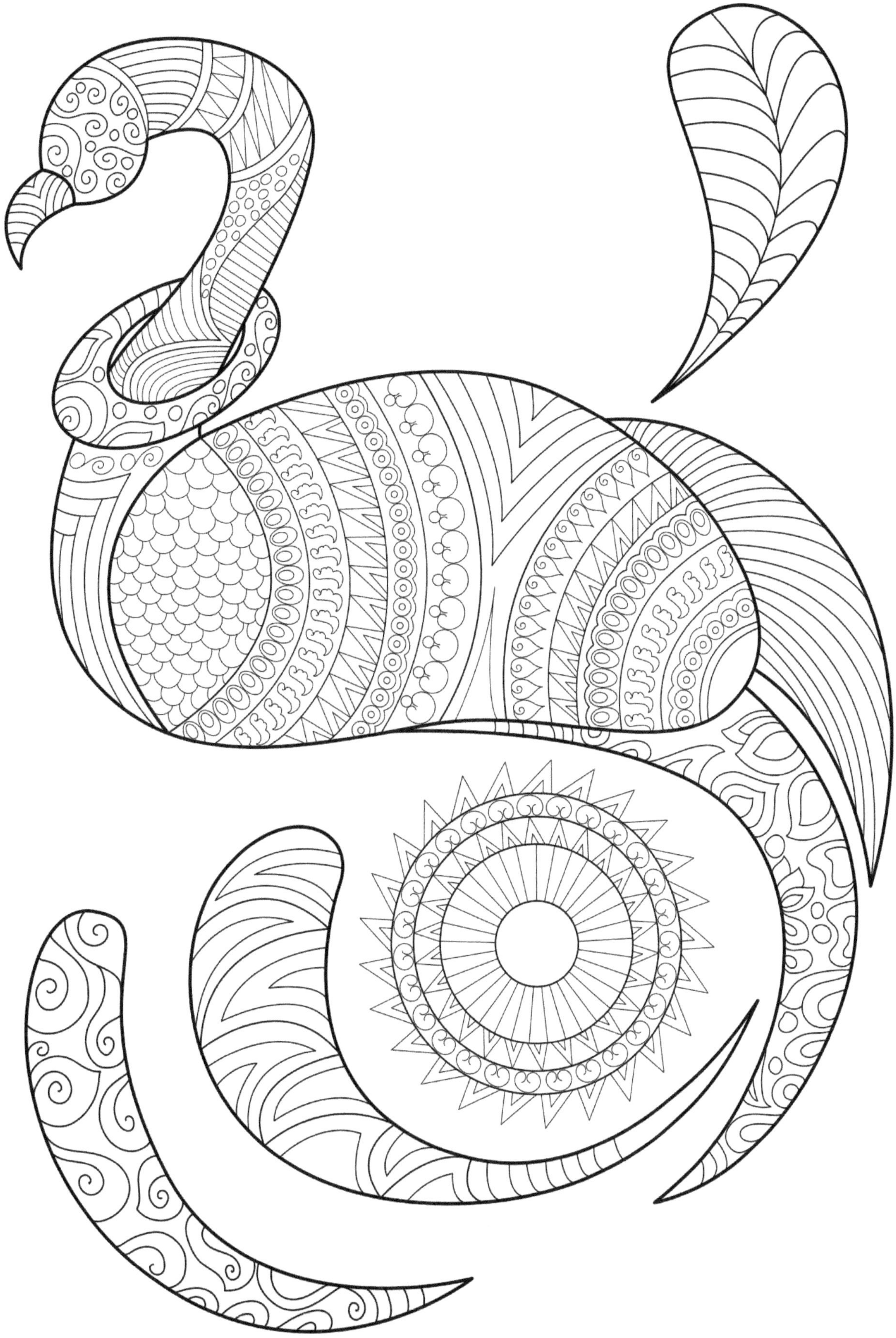

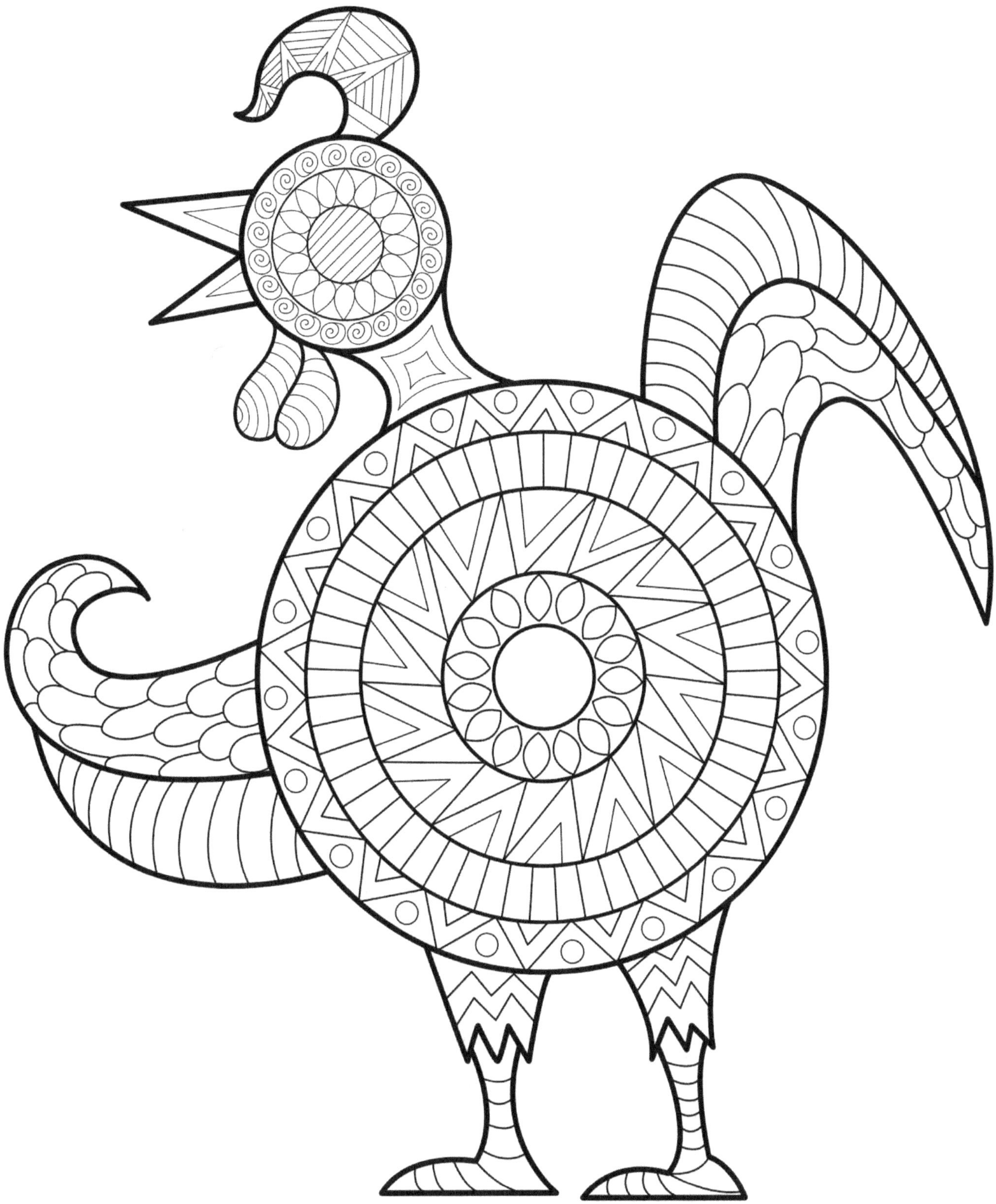

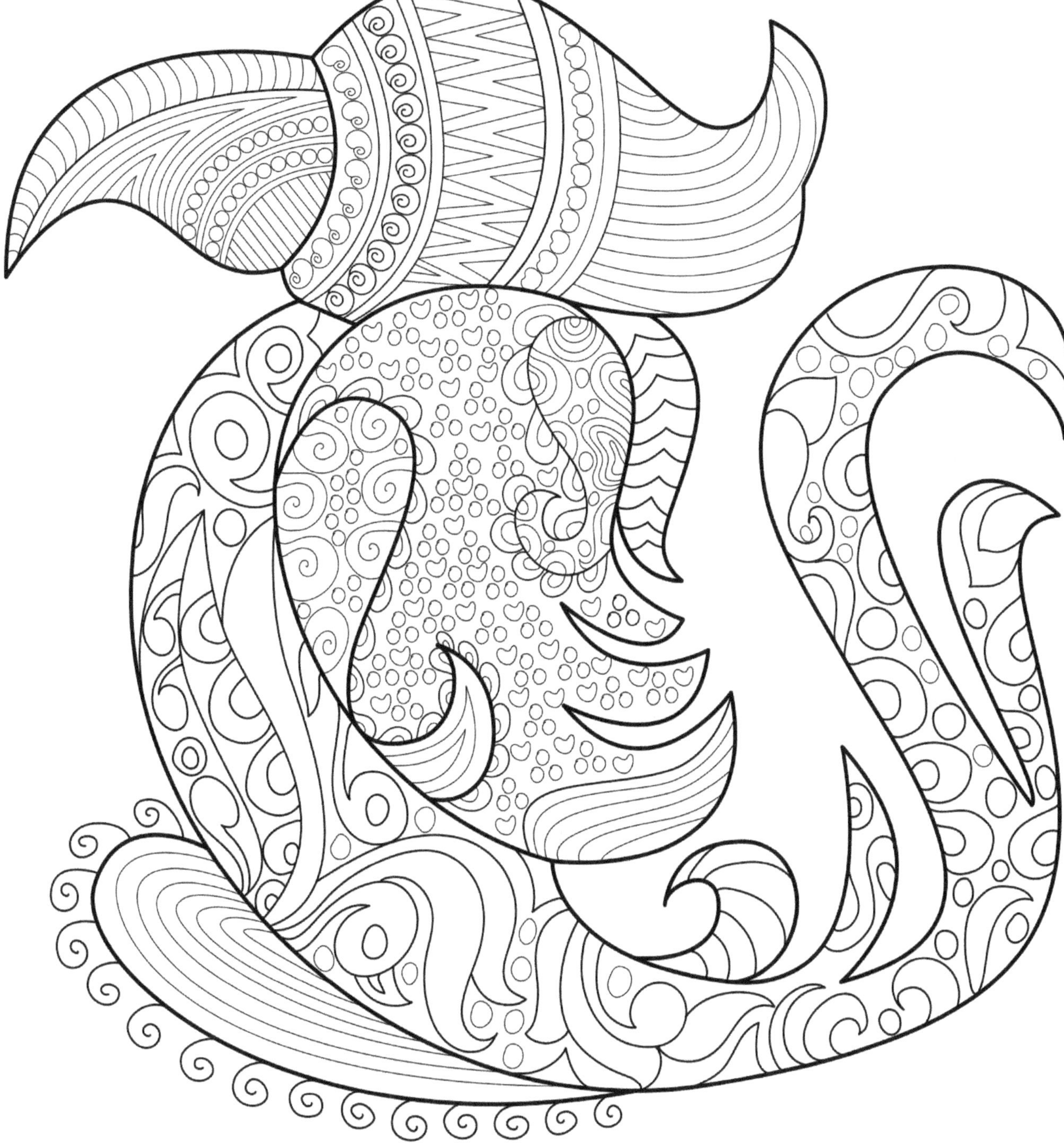

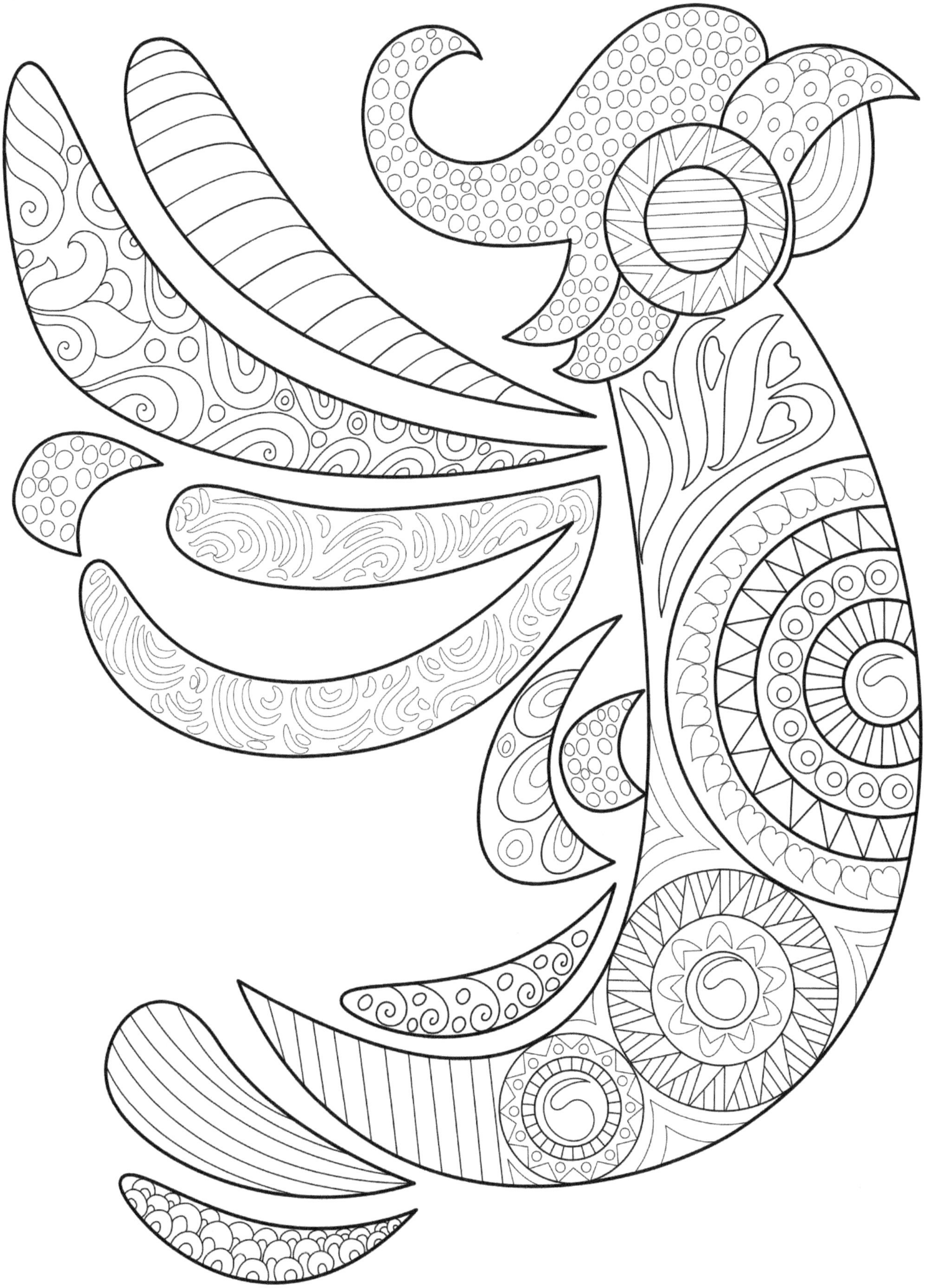

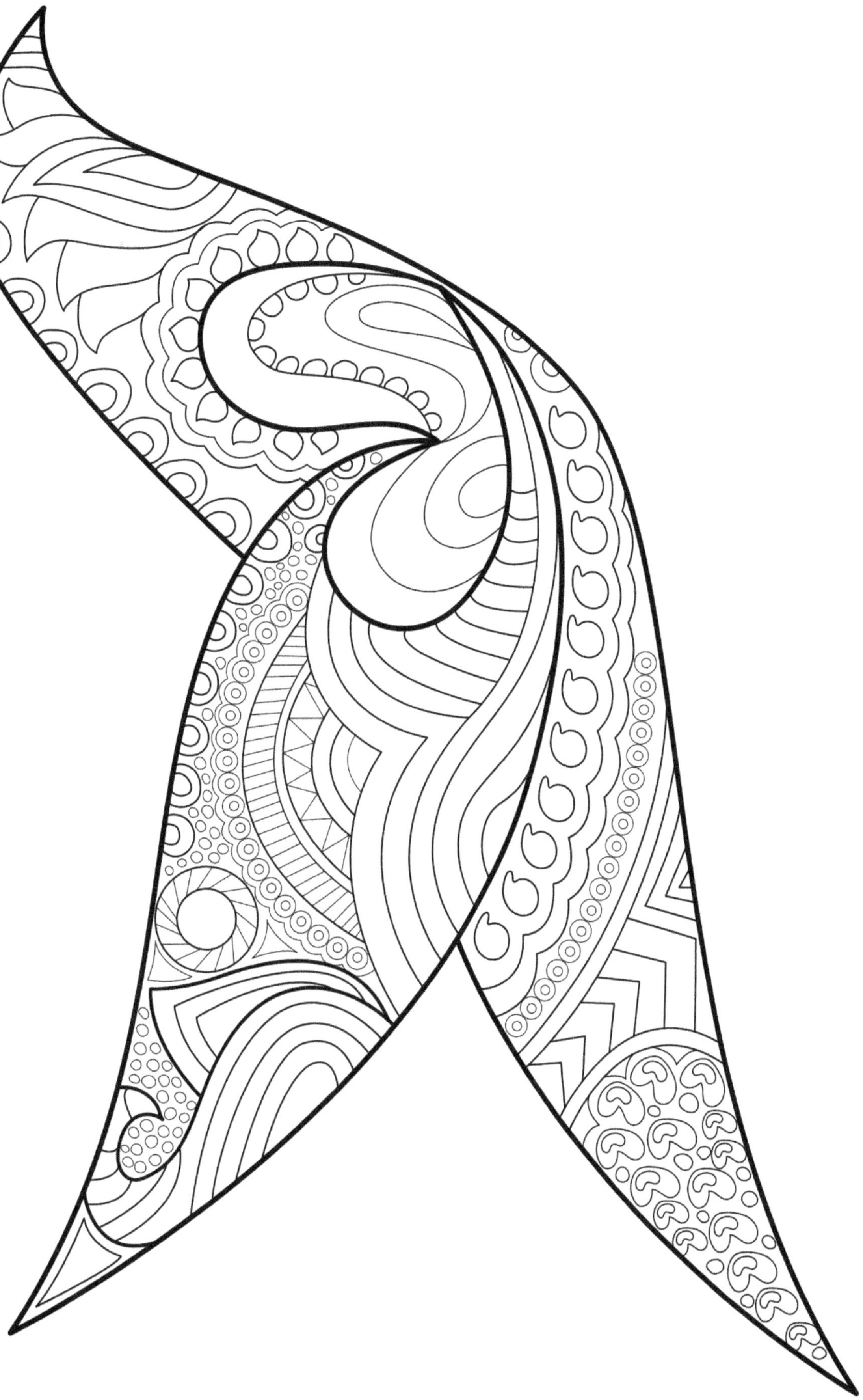

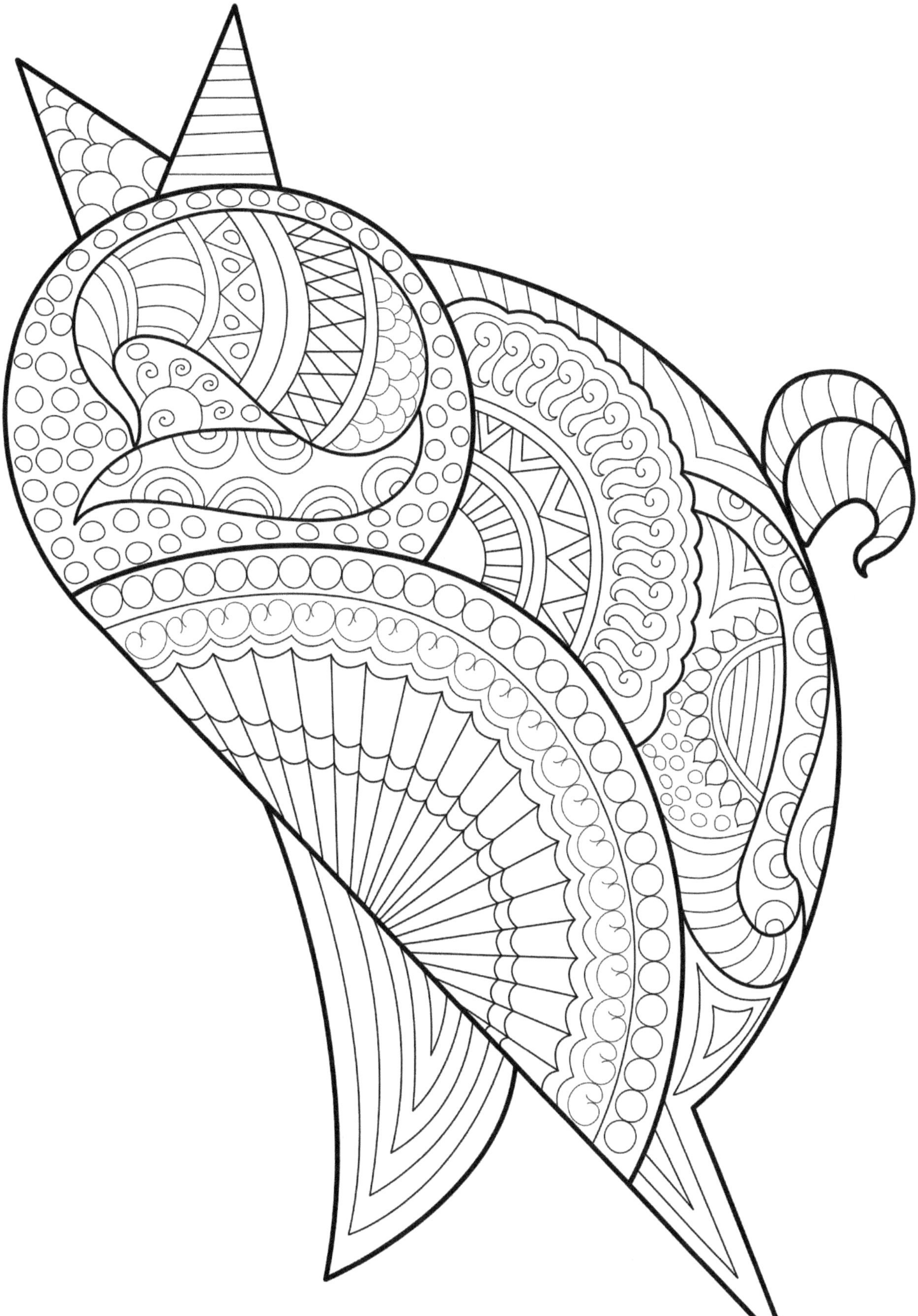

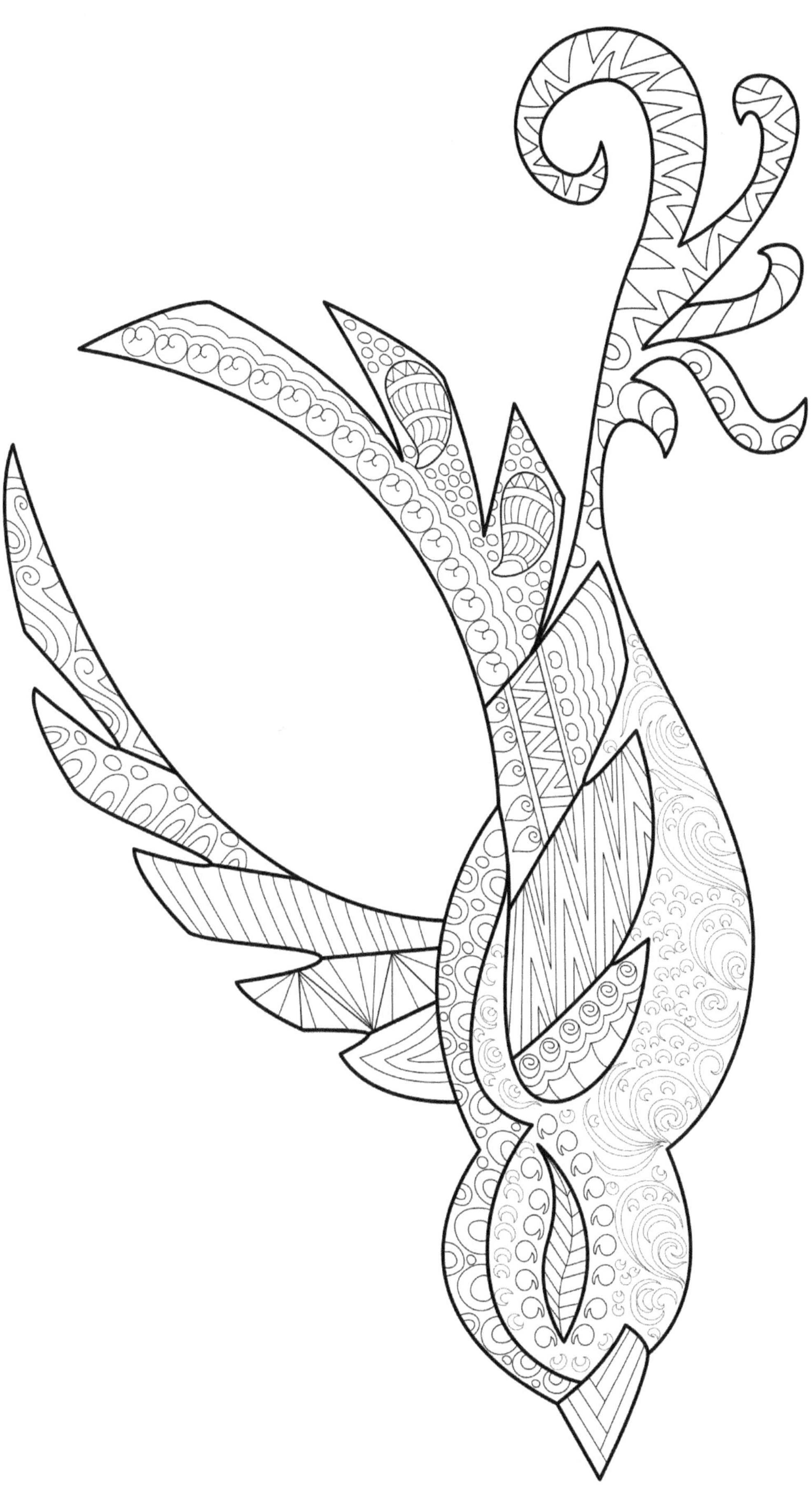

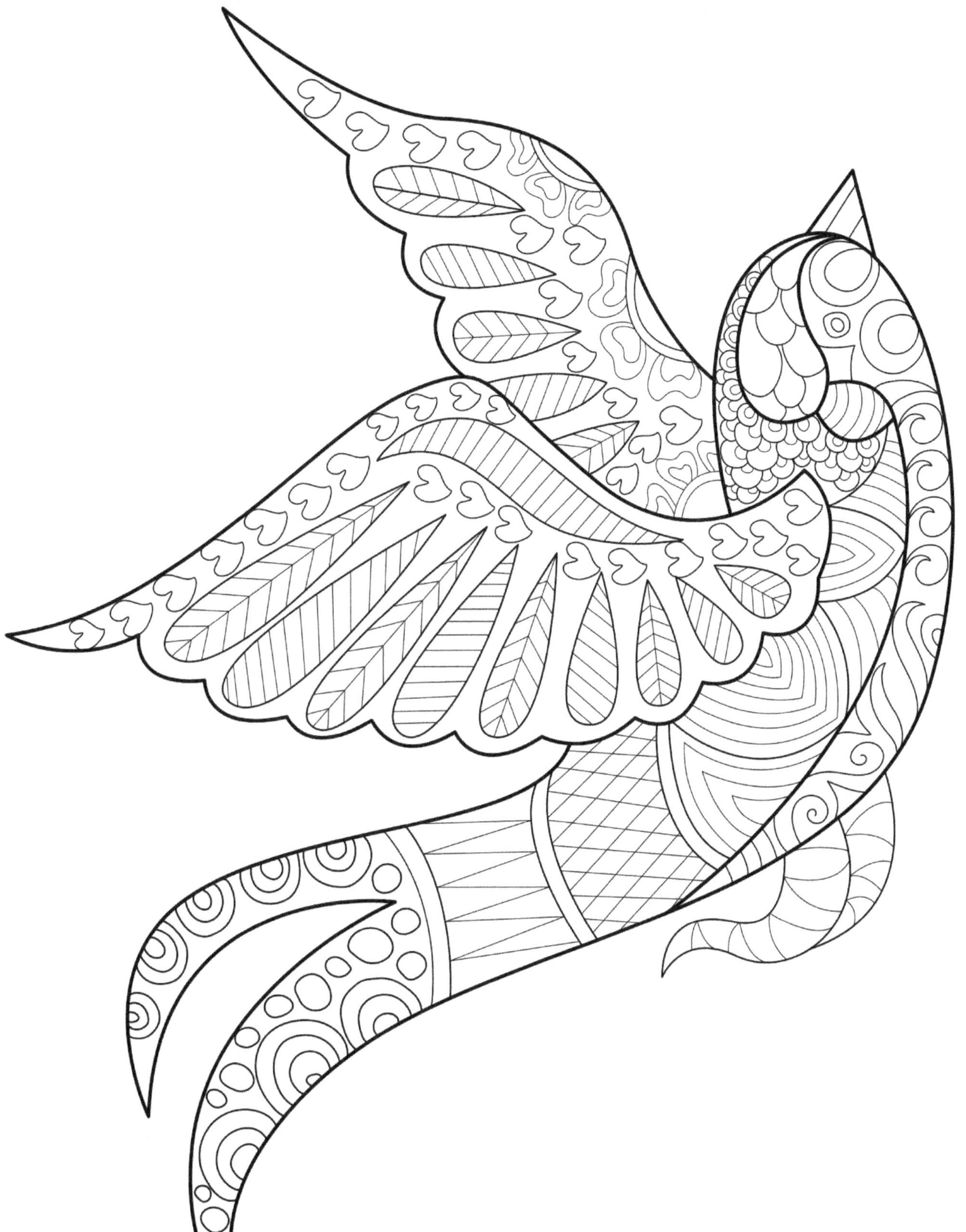

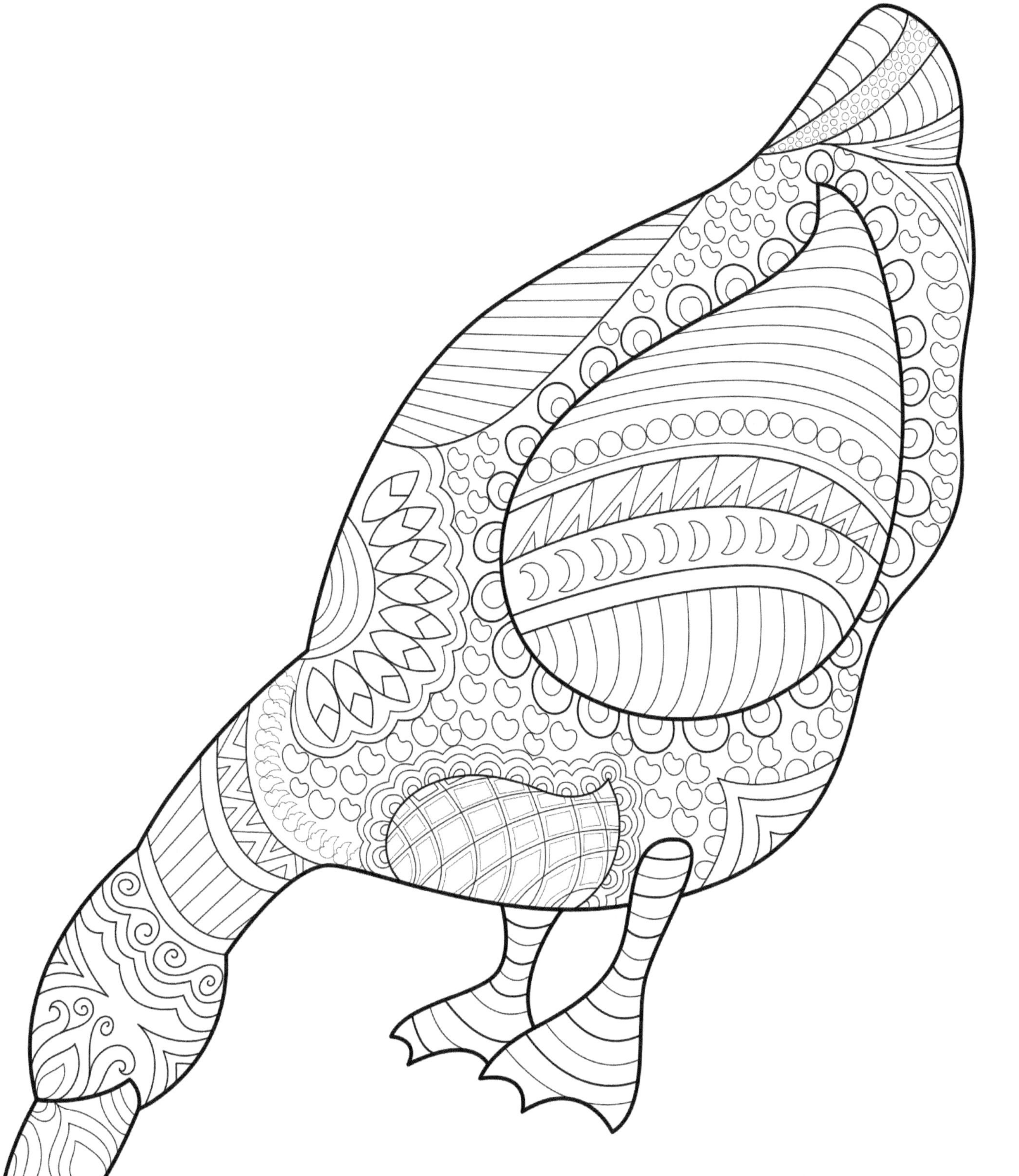

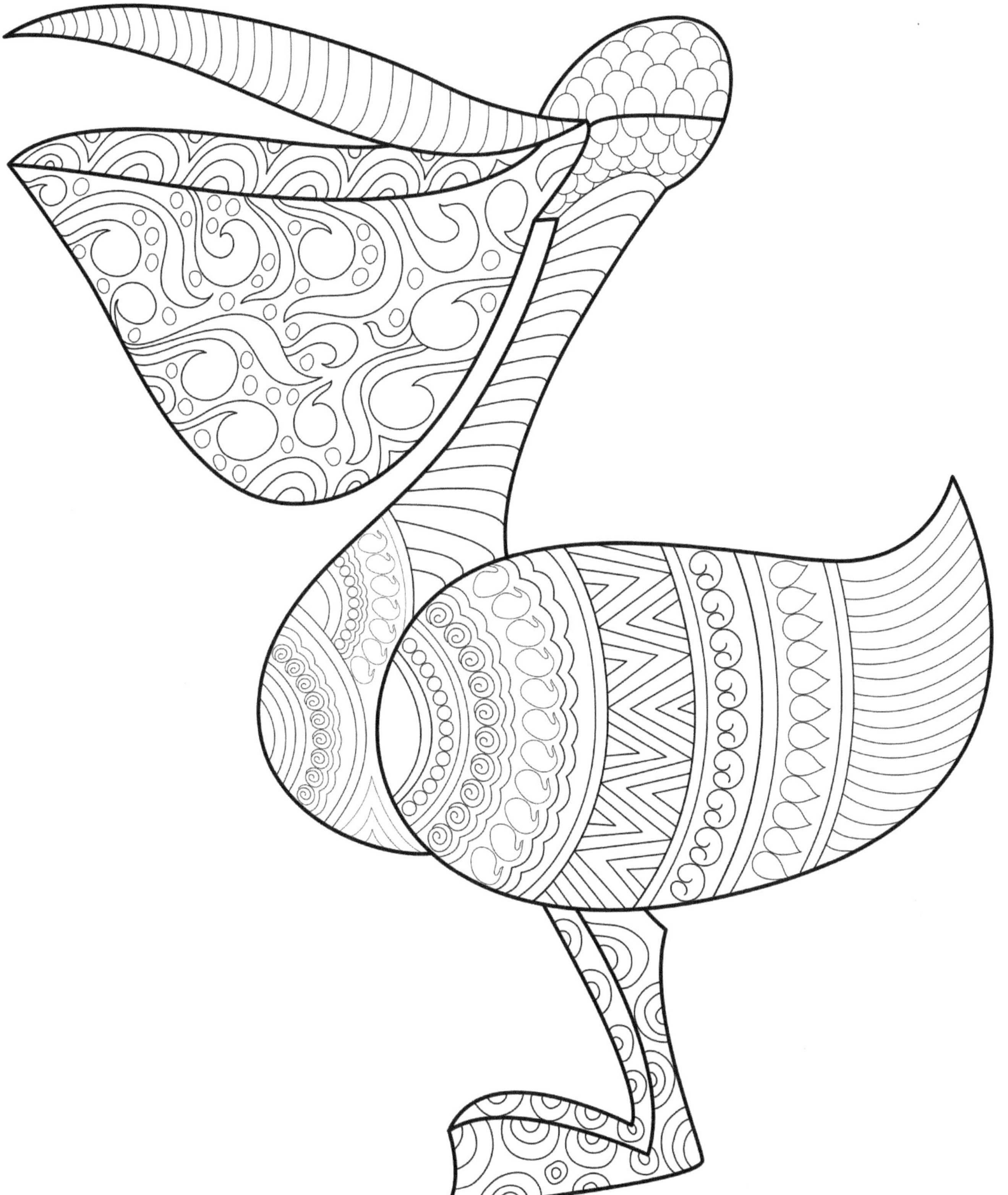

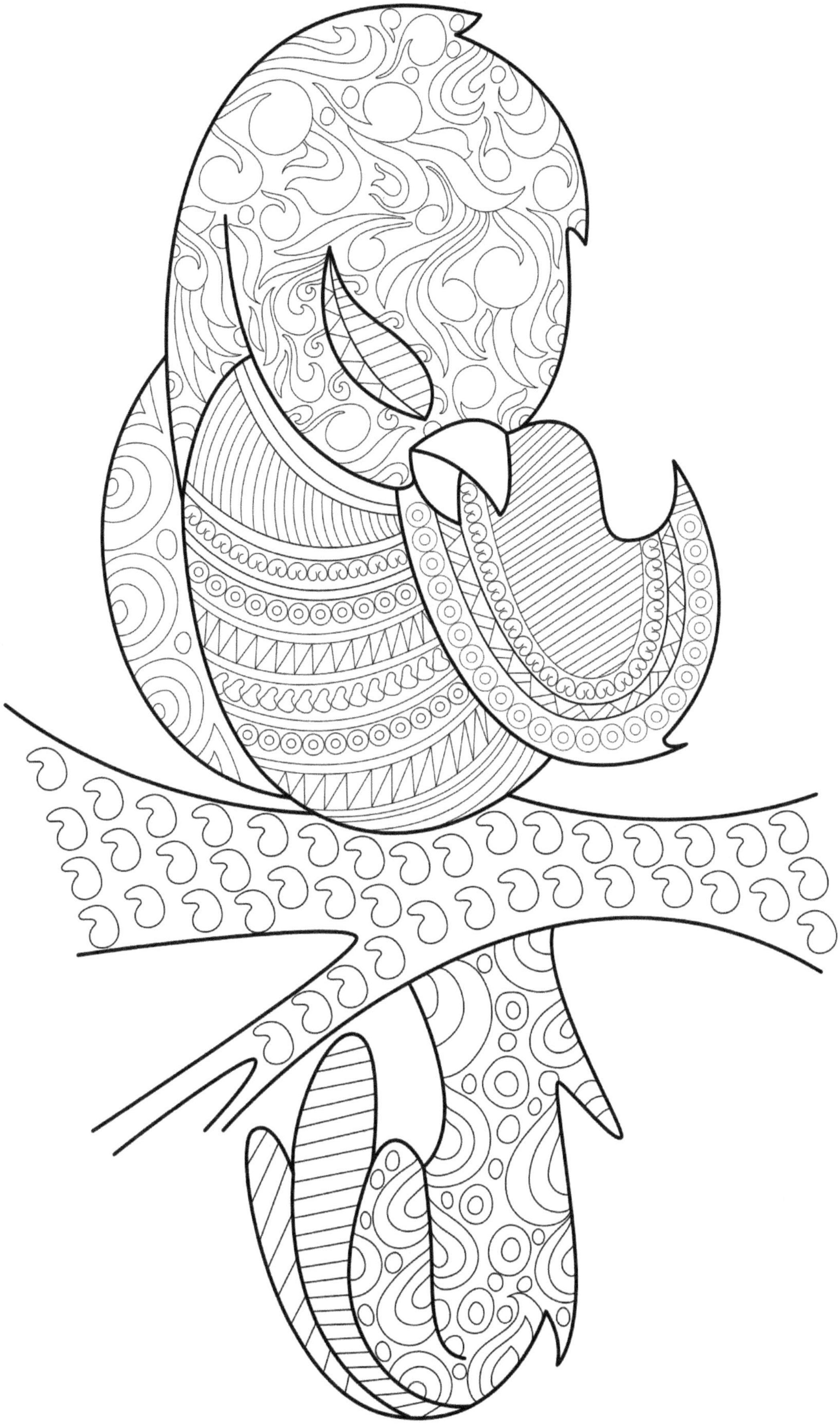

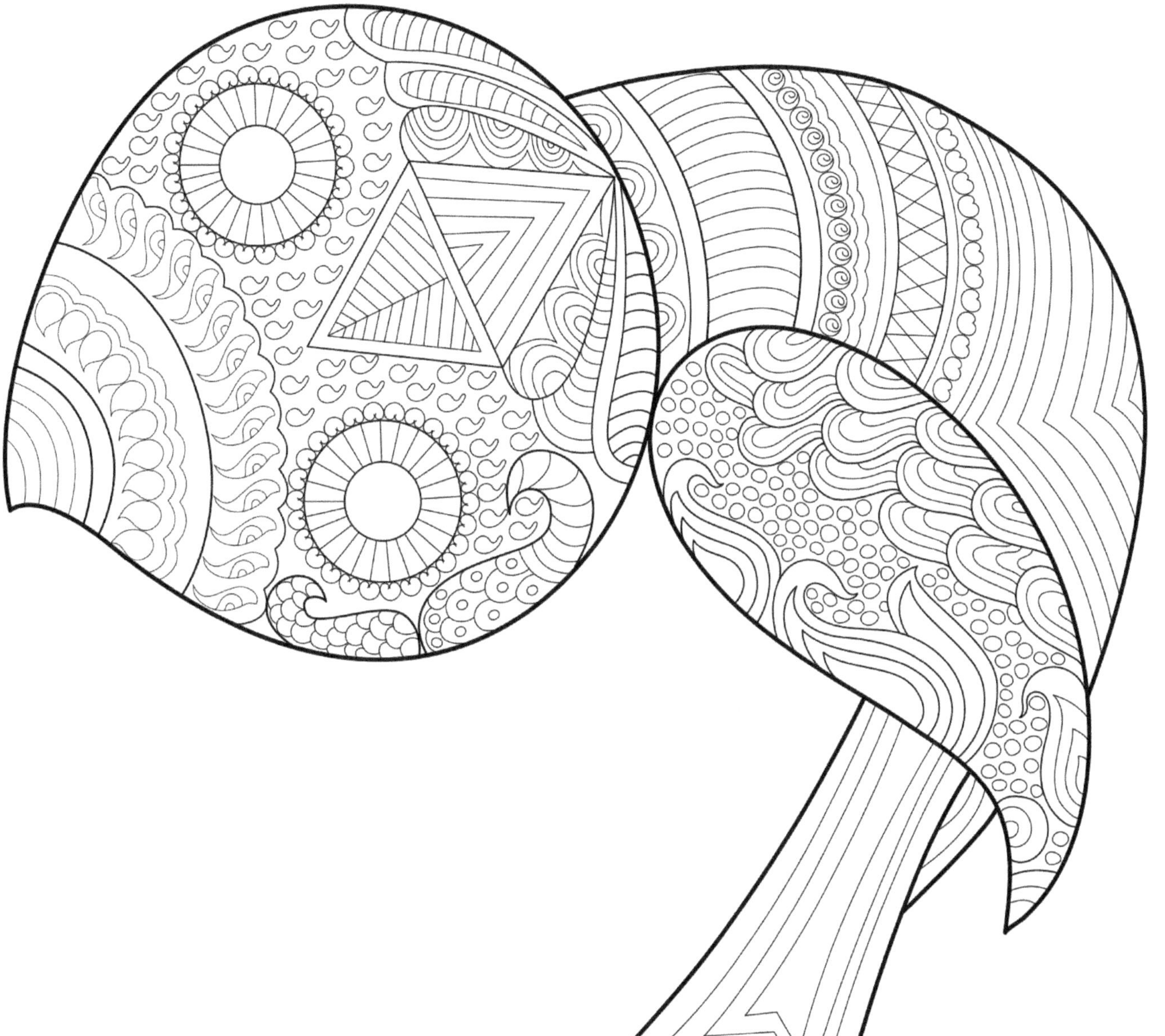

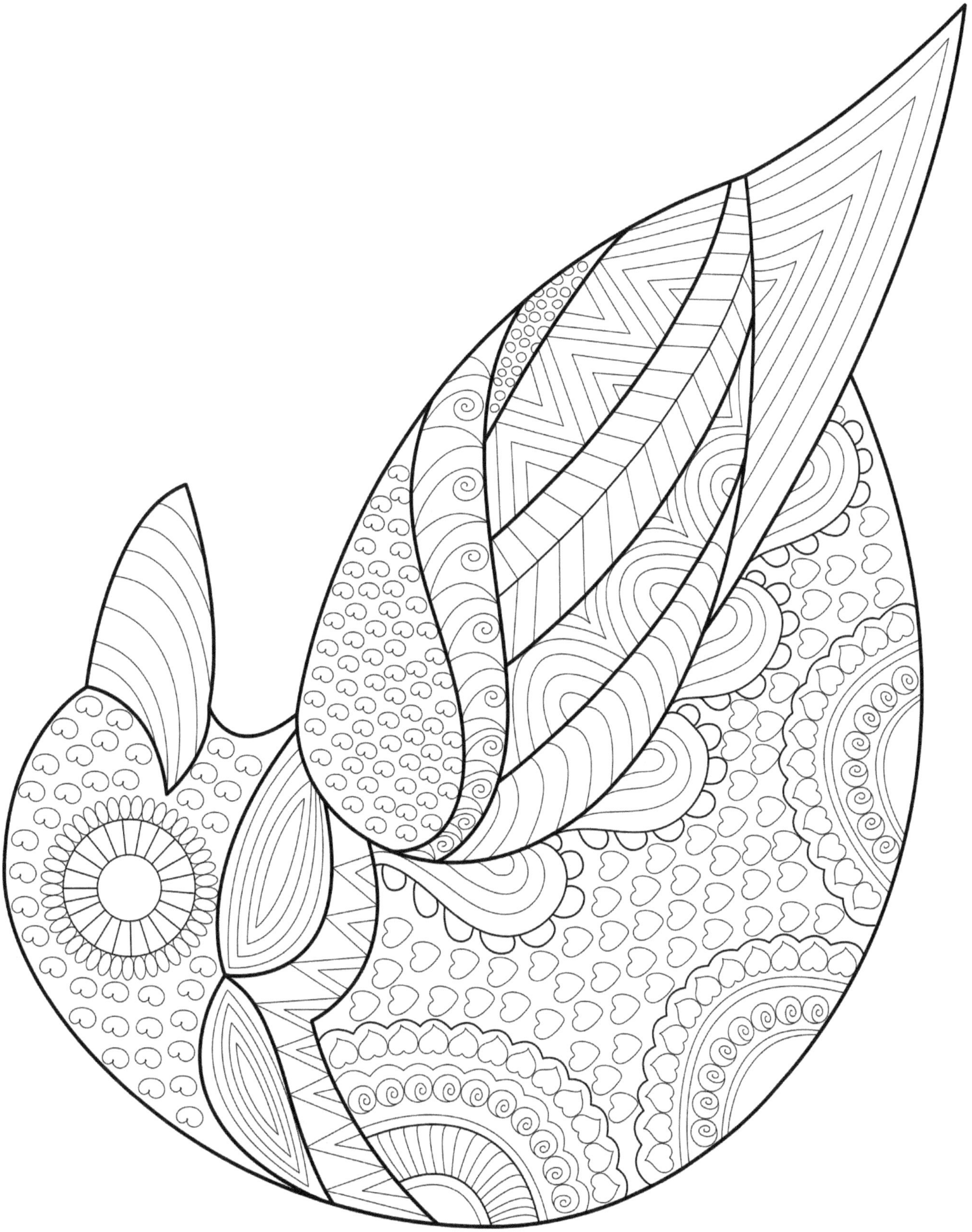

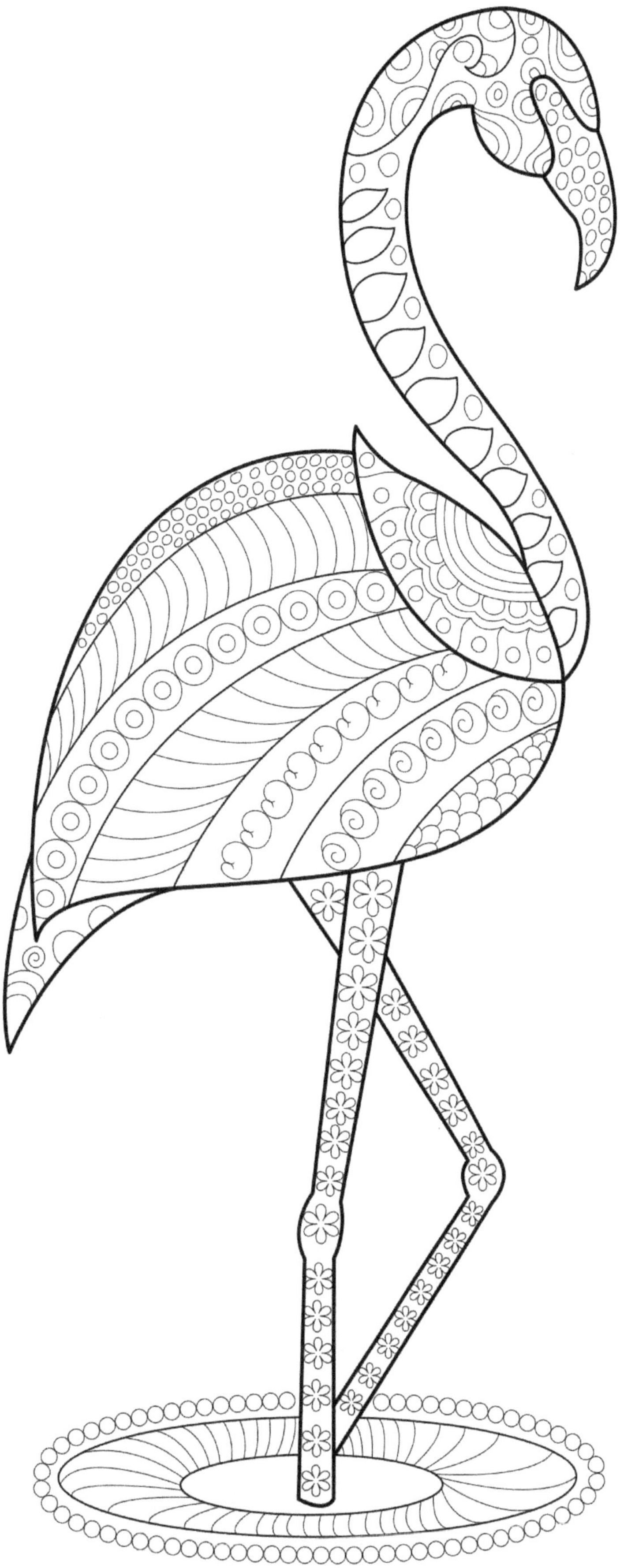

www.ingramcontent.com/pod-product-compliance
Lightning Source LLC
Chambersburg PA
CBHW060442220526
45465CB00008B/3236
* 9 7 9 8 6 4 4 5 6 8 2 9 1 *